AF223978

CREATION AND CONTROL OF A SMALL BUSINESS

A step-by-step simple guide for first-time entry to the business sphere.

John L. Bates

CONTENTS

CHAPTER 1

INTRODUCTION

Many small businesses, of all variations and differing disciplines, are created every year, every one without exception, with excitement and positive ambitions and dreams. Are you one of these? Many of these embryo businesses fail within the first twelve months, and many more during the next two to five years. Less than 2% are still active and, therefore, probably successful after twenty years—that is, only two out of every hundred. If you are suspicious or don't quite believe this statement, check out the statistics.

The US Small Business Administration has seen lots of small businesses come and, unfortunately, go. According to the US SBA statistical information, over 50% of small businesses fail in the first five years. Why? What goes wrong?

In his book *Small Business Management*, Michael Ames gives the following reasons for the failure of small businesses:
1. Lack of experience
2. Insufficient capital (money)
3. Poor location
4. Poor inventory management
5. Over-investment in fixed assets
6. Poor credit arrangements
7. Personal use of business funds
8. Unexpected growth

Gustav Berle adds two more reasons in his *Do It Yourself Business Book*:

1. Competition
2. Low sales

Of course, all these are genuine reasons for failure if not addressed and then addressed correctly. They are all subjects that exist and are not intended to frighten you. You will discover that there are several more to consider. You must be prepared for the rocky path ahead. Underestimating the difficulty of starting a business is one of the biggest obstacles entrepreneurs face. However, success can be yours if you are patient, willing to work hard, and take all the necessary steps.

This book will guide you through the seemingly difficult steps outlined in the foregoing and through many others that may prove challenging.

On the Upside

It's true that there are many reasons in society, warning us not to start our own business. But for the right person, and the right reasons, the advantages of business ownership far outweigh the risks.

You will be your own boss. Hard work and long hours will directly benefit you, rather than increase profits for someone else. Earning and growth potential are far greater. A new venture isas exciting as it is risky. Running a business provides endless challenges and opportunities for learning.

But initially, money must not be the prime motivator. Get the job done, and money will follow.

And yet there should be no real reason for any abject failure in the realisation of one's dreams. The following chapters will assist you to become a member of the 2%, providing you are disciplined and are prepared to give the time, devotion, and flexible innovation in laying a suitable and substantial foundation. The more planning and preparation done initially, the more it will help to sustain the long-term viability of your business.

Now that you have decided to create your own successful business, you must be aware that many before you have craved the same ambition, but only a very few have succeeded in the long-term. Most fall by the wayside, with disastrous effects. These effects include bankruptcy, loss of dignity, broken homes, lost families, reliance on government handouts and so on. But most of these disasters can be, and should have been, avoided by developing, creating, and following, to the letter, a simple plan and religiously adhering to its dictates. You must exhibit sufficient discipline of self-control to plan your entry into the business sphere to the finest point of detail. This is not difficult but needs self-discipline. Positive thinking is an absolute and non-negotiable requirement, and any negative beliefs and pessimism you may harbour must be cast aside. You will need to spend many hours in analysis, review, planning, and extensive research. Dream a little, and use a crystal ball, influenced by available facts. All these are necessary for positive forecasting. Family, friends, acquaintances, and others may criticise and cast doubts on your beliefs, causing you to reconsider and, perhaps, change your plans. Remember, they will not be there for you later when, during business activities, difficult times occur. And believe me, difficult times will happen, and your planning now, together with the ongoing control of your business, will keep these difficult times to a minimum. The planning of your business is your function and responsibility, and your success will depend upon your motivation and positive beliefs. Lastly, document all your plans as you develop them and be prepared at all times to go back and amend the detail, regardless of how much effort is required to rework the dependant analyses.

The reasons for failure are many, and most of these are rarely acknowledged as the personal fault of the business owner. Many times, it is claimed, often falsely, that some outside force has caused the failure. These forces are often identified as unfair competition, government pressures, bank and financier seemingly excessively strict and unfair conditions, bureaucratic requirements, clients' unrealistic demands, staff disloyalty, economic conditions, international market fluctuations, and many more. These may all contribute, but on most occasions, none is the real cause of failure. Although they may have had some influence and may, in the cause of self- preservation and protectionism, be recognised as the major causes of failure, they are merely contributing factors. Failure can almost always be placed directly upon unprofessionalism and poorly executed actions or lack of actions by the owner. Rarely will this be recognised as an admission of personal failure, and in all the businesses with which I have been either directly involved or with whom I have consulted in an endeavour to save them from closure, there has always been a valid reason for all adverse and acceptable business happenings. Almost always, this imaginary validity can be traced back to poor planning, poor and irresponsible practices, and insufficient control and responsibility by the owner.

Failure can be due to many and varied reasons. The following are some of them, to name a few:

- Lack of dedication and belief.
a) Using business cash for private use without record. This is recognised colloquially as 'dipping into the till'.
b) Absence of, or variation from, a predetermined, focused Strategic Plan and Mission Statement.
c) Distraction from the carefully considered directional business 'Vision'.
d) Unwilling to apply the work ethics and long hours that are required. Personal time invested into a business cannot be measured in terms of missed reimbursement.

e) Refusal to delegate as the business grows. When the business successfully expands, and the staff are employed to cope with the growth, then training, guidance, trust, and delegation must be applied and continually watched and audited closely.

f) Poor operational and expense control. During the initial development, and indeed at all ensuing times, all expense commitments must be closely examined to determine the need before commitment.

- Shortage of cash. This will almost always be an ongoing problem which can be clarified or eased through effective planning such as, 'cash flow' analyses and financial, bank, or other financier assistance. This will be addressed in detail later.

You will have recognised that I have not itemised technical knowledge, or the lack of it, as a reason for failure. Usually, the business prospect is adept technically, and the prospective businessperson's personal expertise is often the encouragement for considering a business in which one is technically capable. Consider a corner store, or a professional service, such as a general practitioner or dentist or similar health provider, or a motor mechanic, or computer technician, or the plethora of other opportunistic business occupations. To consider entry into a business of any discipline, one is usually experienced or qualified in that area. However, I maintain that personal expertise in the chosen subject of business is a minor consideration and completely out-shadowed by the need for business management, planning, expertise, and focused attention. This business guide will, I trust, convince you that the daily planning and control of the management functions of your business will lead you to success, and the technical aspects, whilst important, can be augmented by employees who possess the necessary expertise. The old adage is quite true. You will lose control of the important daily and future functions of your business if you are always deeply involved in the technical activity of your business.

There can be no real finite reason for failure nor will failure occur through misadventure, if specific disciplinary procedures are followed with dedication and logical simplicity. So let this be the last reference to 'failure' during your study of this guide and, eventually, your search for a successful business with ongoing success.

CHAPTER 2

THINK ABOUT IT

The next consideration is financial reward. If your main, initial ambition is to get rich quickly and earn large profits, forget it. For many years during the creation and development of my business, my staff earned more take-home money than I pocketed as my salary. Get the job done right first and develop your business, and rewards will eventually come. If you draw unauthorised or unrecorded cash for private use, this is another quick slide to the loss of control and subsequent closure. If you let business expenses flow out of control without a 'Scrooge control' mentality, you will not achieve your operational results. You must be prepared to control this discipline effectively, and the following chapters will guide you in a simple procedure to achieve ultimate success. Indeed, this guide might also be applied to your private finances and budgets, enabling you to control your own private destiny financially. Do not mix the two. Business and private financial control must be separate entities.

The whole exercise of business planning and development can be exciting, rewarding, interesting, and fun. But always remember to be professional and accept that you are the 'boss'. Hard decisions have to be made from time to time. Team involvement is great, but the buck stops with you, and the ultimate responsibility will always come back to you, not the team. And, of course, identify at every level of your business, who is the customer, internally and externally, and remember that the external customer must be always considered right whilst the internal customer usually can contribute to your continual improvement policies.

Not if but I hope that when you are successful, many of your relatives, friends, and colleagues will tell you, and generally comment to all and sundry, that you have been lucky. Yes, the harder you are prepared to work, and the harder you plan and audit, the luckier you will get. There is no such thing as pure luck in business. Opportunities may arise from time to time, and it is strange that the more you are involved, the more you network, and the harder and longer you apply yourself, the more opportunities will arise.

You must be prepared to network and make yourself known to the right people and organisations. This will involve memberships of influential business organisations, attendance and involvement at industry meetings, and after-hour's network relationships with related organisations, thus providing a growing listing of business acquaintances. Always utilise business cards as a means of being known among the various industry associates. Be prepared to become involved in community affairs, thus gaining valuable connections. Excellent service, excellent quality, and attention to the requirements of the client are also among practical forms of networking. Immediate results of networking invariably do not occur, and one can easily become disenchanted with the seeming waste of time. But results will come at, perhaps, the most unexpected time. And gradually, you will become known and respected.

CHAPTER 3

LOOK FORWARD, NOT BACK

Contrary to popular belief, I do not consider competitors and their activities to be of extreme importance and, therefore, should be primarily unworthy of your extensive analysis. Many business proprietors and senior managers are possessed with the need to identify and follow their competitor's progress. When they can rapidly draw level with their competitors, they consider themselves and their business as successful. This is negative thinking and will never enable a rise to profitable leadership. Energy that may be put into this in-depth competitor analysis can adversely affect the energy you would, or should, give to your own business progress. Naturally, you must be aware of your competitors and their activities, but never become obsessed and follow them to the most detailed degree. I always encouraged my clients to look ahead and move forward, rather than look into the rear-view mirror. The positive concept of this philosophy, of course, is that your business will always be ahead of your competitors in all your planning and daily operations. Naturally, there may be times that you want to understand where you stand in relation to the industry leaders, and you may want to identify with the range of products they market and the product innovation they may apply. However, don't let this knowledge or research take your eye off the ball. It is not important when compared to your own progress. For example, say you opened a delicatessen, and Woolworths or Coles or any other of the large supermarket chains, are in near proximity. There is no point in worrying about their activities. You will never compete, so develop your own strategy and, preferably, one that they cannot emulate. Think about it. There are many opportunities that large businesses cannot apply, that may be readily applicable for a small business and attractive to the customers. More particularly, those large businesses, realising that they are your competitors, will, hopefully, spend their time emulating your activities and not necessarily concentrating on their own development.

Enjoy small marketing forays into their activities, thus letting them know that you are there and will compete. Solicit their customers, invariably finding some dissatisfaction among them, and identify those who are willing to change to your services, for a trial. The cries of unfair trading, of immoral solicitation of their database, and threats of legal action will all take their eye off the ball, leaving you to bask in an increased client base of your own. Naturally, you must exercise care in this regard, always withdrawing at the strategic time with appropriate apologies, thus avoiding any legal retribution.

CHAPTER 4
BUSINESS ELEMENTS

There are many aspects of business, other than the technical requirements necessary, to satisfy the client. All these aspects are addressed in detail later and are merely shown here as an introduction to those areas that are among the most important factors for your success. Note that technical and professional expertise is not included and is left to your discretion whether this is a major item for detailed consideration. Remember that you can always employ or contract technical and professional expertise. If you are technically expert in the particular field of operation that you have chosen for your business, and you concentrate on this discipline, you may adversely affect the many more important facets of business development and operation, resulting in the eventual collapse of your business.

So what are the elements for creation and ongoing development?

- **Product**. What are the products or services you intend to provide? This must be the first determination. Don't even consider moving on until you decide on the type of business you intend to create. I have had clients contract me to help them establish a business, and when questioned, they had no idea what business or product they intended to engage. All they wanted was to become a business owner and get rich quick. I encouraged them to rethink their position. Some who ignored this advice and either acquired or created a business without the all-essential planning and preparation lasted only a short time with eventual financial devastation. This avalanche of loss usually carries many other valued assets with it, such as family and friends.

- **Vision**. Determine the future direction and achievements to which you and your business will aspire. Consider the ensuing five years. Any longer and you may need a fortune teller. This 'Vision' of yours will lay the foundation for all your activities. It will dictate the need to always work and make decisions towards the attainment of this Vision. Every business decision made by you, and subsequently by your staff during daily operational decision- making, must be guided by and lead in the same direction as this Vision. This is an exciting exercise and one that you should not arrive at quickly or without in-depth consideration. The Vision should not necessarily involve expansion and development, although positive thinking would lead to this conclusion. It may be that you consider downsizing the acquired business; this needs to be documented as part of your 'Vision'. It doesn't necessarily require an increasing and expanding business to take over all others but may mean a downsizing and specific market focus.

- **Mission Statement**. This is a flow on from your Vision but should address the more detailed ensuing twelve months and expected achievements, all moving towards your eventual Vision. This Plan should be more definitive, and all your business activities during these twelve months must be directed towards the achievement of this Mission Statement. Regular reviews will highlight whether this is being achieved or needs amendment or needs a more targeted effort. Associates, customers, and service providers should all be made aware of your Mission Statement. It, therefore, serves as a marketing tool.

- **Business Location**. Where will you establish your business? Many aspects have to beconsidered before this decision is made. This is an important element and one that will require some research. If you are acquiring an existing business, it is probable that the location is already fixed as the existing situation. It is difficult, although not impossible, to change business addresses along the way after you have commenced trading. Have you ever noticed where the leading fast food outlets are situated? It is not by chance that they are clustered together or that they are all on a main road. All these aspects are the result of extensive research.

- Working from home can be an unnecessary cross to bear, although inexpensive. It can lead to stress and frustration, including a public perception of a small, ineffective, poor profile. Even if you are creating a small, one-person service business, which could effectively operate from your home, it is still advisable to establish and locate in a separate situation. Obviously, home operation can be less expensive and, perhaps, more convenient, but there are many negatives that come with a home-based operation. I will guide you in this decision. Much will depend, but not entirely, on the product, type, and size of business that you plan.

- **Local Government Approvals**. These may be required, and now is the time to think about that. Be acutely aware of the need for local government involvement. Reference to them at this early stage can save a lot of inconvenience and expense at a later date. These government bodies can be not only a useful and strong colleague but also a devastating adversary. Should you move or act without reference to the authorities, they can be an exacting interference at a later time, causing much stress and expense. These authorities may appear to be over-demanding, but they have a purpose and can demonstrate excessive admonishments if ignored.

- **Marketing**. How will you become known in the community? When, where, and how will you advertise, if at all? Much will depend on the area of business, location, size, and vision you have chosen. Hence the need to sequence your planning in logical order, as explained herein. What you can afford, although in the initial stages, be frugal. Your efforts need not be entirely guided by your available cash. There are many marketing strategies that are effective and inexpensive. Alternatively, there are many that appear attractive at first glance but are expensive and less effective. However, it will be necessary to invest in this discipline, and detailed explanation and guidance will come later. Marketing is of utmost importance to your success and must be considered accordingly. It is not sufficient to produce a good product or service and leave it to the potential customers to identify with you and to want to buy your product or service. You must seek them out and 'sell' yourself and your product. Even after you have established and enjoy some aspect of a permanent customer base, you must continue to advertise and promote.

- **Operations, Service Centres, Activity.** How will this be done, and what staffing is necessary? Consider the need for staff and the minimum number required, what expertise will be required, and the need for training, client service, procedures, and policy requirements. It may be that you want staff uniforms. You will need documented procedures. The development of documented procedures must have the details of how, where, and what, using the principle of formal, although simple, written procedures. All focused functions must be described, adopting a formal documentation procedure. This development will establish uniform operational methods for all to apply, thus providing quality of product and service for the client. These procedures will also provide an essential medium for training and ongoing auditing of staff practices to ensure all within your business, including yourself, are applying a uniform and standard operation. This will leadto a necessary 'Continuous Improvement' strategy and ultimate quality of product and operation. The most effective programme for quality improvement, expense control with subsequent profitability, and improved customer service is through this method of Continuous Improvement or

Complaint Investigation. These procedures will be changed from time to time as the need for improvement of operation is identified.

- **Innovation.** You must always consider the continuing development and improvement of your product range. Most products and services should be subject to regular review and amendment/change in order to maintain client attraction. Innovation, conducted formally, can be a major source of quality improvement and cost reduction. A regular review of your product and/or service, endeavouring to establish a less complicated and less expensive procedure or design whilst maintaining or even, and preferably, increasing the effectiveness and quality aspect is not only possible but an accepted manner of continuous improvement in business.

- **External Consultants.** Will you require external assistance such as a professional accountant? It is often financially beneficial to use an external accountant for operational results, periodical financial reviews, and end-of-year taxation requirements. A reputable accountant can be a valuable adviser with whom confidentiality can be assumed. Consider also the need, either now or in the future, for a legal service. Consider also, at this time, the need for other professional expertise and advice that may not be practical on a full-time basis within your business. Perhaps there may be an associate or reputable business adviser who would be willing to act as a non-executive director or merely a valuable mentor. Care must be exercised in using these valuable mediums. All are conscious of legal mitigation and, therefore, will be loath to advise any form of risk, whereas you as the owner must adopt considered risk at times in order to advance.

- **Business Disciplines.** Accreditation to selected and relevant international standards, such as formal accreditation for Quality, Environmental, and Occupational Health and Safety (OH&S) standards, may be an advantage to consider. There may be some marketing and operational value in adopting

'Standard' conformances. Some International Standards may be essential to provide for the opportunity to achieve business and governmental acceptance of your product. Study the relevant Standard carefully and apply its demands sensibly and without the overkill of bureaucratic procedures. Many businesses adopt 'over the top' conformances to the requirements of a Standard, thinking that the applicable assessors will respect this attention to detail. Mostly, it is unnecessary, and excessive expensive can be incurred in being overzealous in this area.

- **Product Cost**. As vague as it may seem at this time, you must consider the total cost of your product or service. This will involve the cost of purchase of services, componentry, final product, cost of production and/or service, and cost of expenses, including overhead costs. It is a surprisingly strange yet factual situation that many business creators are not aware of their true product and service costs. They, therefore, cannot accurately determine sales pricing and subsequent profitability. Often, the sale price of a product or service is determined merely by matching or cutting the competitor's pricing. This is done with dire results and can lead quickly to loss of profit. You must be aware, and always remember, that any loss of profit is lost cash, never to be redeemed. Research carried out at this time will save much valuable time later and provide accurate loss saving estimates.

- **Margins**. In addition to the foregoing 'product cost', which will include overhead recovery or the recovery of expenses, how much margin and profit do you require? This must besufficient to provide for you personally, in addition to your salary, and for ongoing business development and personal accumulation of profit. This, coupled with the total product cost, represents the total base price of your product/ service. Adjustments for additional profit or for the cost of more aggressive market penetration can be effected, whilst considering the true effect on the sales volume if the price is varied up or down.

- **Review and Amendment**. Your policy regarding ongoing management style must include a regular review of the expenses, overheads, margins, and profit. Any variation from the planned results must be addressed and, if necessary, the plans amended. A regular review of your trading Profit and Loss Statements will reveal any weaknesses that need correcting. An annual review is not sufficient as problems can become unmanageable well before the twelve months have expired. I recommend at least quarterly, although a monthly financial review is best, remembering that time is a valuable factor and that monthly reviews, whilst valuable, take up your time.

Documentation. The entire planning function must be documented and will consist mainly of—

- strategic plan
- product/service
- vision statement
- mission statement
- business plan
- financial plan

Each of these will be detailed later; they constitute the most important section for development.

Action Plan

An Action Plan is determined from a regular review of all your planning functions. What needs to be done within a time frame and by whom? This needs regular review in order to ensure that actions that need to be carried out are done. If the staff are involved in the business, it can be an effective strategy to include them in this review of the Action Plan. An Action Plan can be established and regularly reviewed in conjunction with the essential regular review of your Strategic Plan, Business Plan, and Financial Plan. As other necessities for regular consideration are identified, they must be included in the Action Plan.

Corrective Action

A Corrective Action plan, formally implemented, will ensure that problems and complaints, errors and omissions, and suggestions for improvement are addressed in due time and correction action applied. This is a proven method to realise an ongoing continuing improvement in the business activities, improved quality, and satisfied clientele. Indeed, an effective Corrective Action programme will ensure a continual improvement, constant movement towards improved quality, and profitability.

Disaster Plan

A Disaster Plan should be formulated soon after the business is operational. Many a business could have been saved were the problems highlighted soon enough and professional remedies applied. Recognition and honesty are necessary in the identification of imminent problems, and the courage to face those problems and apply corrective action must apply without recrimination. Although it may seem too late, and you may consider that nothing can be done, you must address how you can save your failing organisation or protect against absolute disaster. Many businesses have experienced this and have either survived or have lost everything. There seems to be no mid-range result. This chapter will walk you through the steps to take in an endeavour to resurrect, save, or protect personal assets in the face of pending business failure.

All these disciplines must be documented as you develop them, ideally using a computer program. Consider using Microsoft Office Word and Excel programs although other competitive computer programs are equally effective. However, many Strategic Plans, Business Plans, Operational and Financial Budgets have been successfully developed and subjected to amendment, using manual methods of basic pencil and paper. Computer programs have simplified this process, particularly in the development of comparable 'what if' alternate plans. It is important that you become familiar with the basics of these functions before you subject them to distanced computer evaluation.

Your finally developed Strategic Plan constitutes your guide for your business operations, and these operations should not be varied without readdressing and, if necessary, amending the Strategic Plan. Governments, banks, financial providers, partners, and other interested parties will favourably accept a formal planning strategy. In all probability, you will need finance in the form of a loan or overdraft, and a formal Strategic Plan will encourage financiers, such as banks, to consider assistance favourably.

Having studied and understood, or rather committed to, all the foregoing, you are ready to commence your Strategic Plan and formal detailed planning for each discipline. Every chapter must be addressed, studied, absorbed, and applied. These following chapters will guide you in every major detail so that when this planning and documentation is complete, and not before, you will be ready to begin a business enterprise and have the best chance for success.

Exciting? Now read on.

CHAPTER 5

PRODUCT AND SERVICE

Identify the product or service you intend to provide. For ease of interpretation, the term 'product', as referenced in this text, will include all business products, services, and other factors you will provide for sale.

What do you intend to create?

- Professional services: Provide professional services? What?
- Manufacture: What? New product or existing?
- Service: Provide a service? If yes, then what type of service—repair or other?
- Transport: What type and area of distribution?
- Wholesale or intermediary sales: Type and area of distribution?
- Retail sales: What type of store?
- Food supply: Retail or wholesale?
- Other.

There are myriad of types of businesses in which you may be involved. All the different types, whatever they may be, will require the same planning. The basic planning and control requirements, as described herein, are essential, whatever the type of business you may contemplate.

All these described activities apply to every type of business.

Consider the marketplace and community acceptance. Is the product or service already available, and is the market sufficiently open to another insurgent? Importation and/or international support must be considered; will this incur international travel? If there is to be international involvement, this will appreciably affect your expense planning. If your business is already a going concern, and the product is established, perhaps your consideration will be only to extend product or service enhancement to encourage client response.

The product may be an innovative item or range of items, in which case it may be advisable to have a professional consultant conduct a market survey, thus establishing a community reaction to your plan and the acceptance of the product. The results of this survey may not return what you want to see. It may be, to some extent, negative and might reveal problems and possible disasters. Actually, an effective survey will contain these flags, not intended to deter your plans or enthusiasm but to make you aware of the problem areas that you should plan to avoid or to combat. You should be suspicious of a survey that does not include warning signals.

Include the survey results into your Strategic Plan.

If the product will involve production procedures, equipment may be required. Identify this equipment, and establish availability and price. Long lead times for procurement may delay your plans for your business commencement. Conversely, the 'used' market may contain suitable equipment for your use at a fraction of the cost of new. New, state-of-the-art, and more efficient and time-saving equipment should be considered as part of a future budget when the business hasbecome established and profitable. There are, of course, arguments against this philosophy, which may be completely credible. Consider whether new equipment may be the prime strategy for the establishment of the business, by having the capability to provide better quality and/ or reduced pricing of the goods than your competitors can supply. However, exercise caution in this decision. Also, alternatively, you might consider, in the early period of development, the acquisition of machined product from contractors. Carry out a 'make or buy' comparison, and you may identify an improved method of supply. This review can be readily applied through the application of a spread sheet, detailing the costs involved in each method that could be adopted, thus providing an avenue for the comparison of results. Then consider any and all external factors combining these with the financial costing results. These external factors may include such influencing subjects as geographical location of contractors, 'just in time' supply, quality of product, reputation of contractors, availability of employees and expertise, should you include production, and the plethora of other affecting aspects, before you finally make your decision. Always be aware, however, in any Make or Buy decisions, you must make provision for overhead recovery. This is the recovery of your internal and other costs. There will be the temptation to buy a product at a certain value, which may be extremely competitive in the market. However, how will your internal costs be paid if you don't add to your purchase costing a factor for recovery of your internal costs? Many businesses have priced product for sale at a price which includes the purchase costs and a factor for profit, but they forget about the internal expense costing. Thus, they find, in rapid time, that all the planned profit is taken up to pay for the business internal costs.

The identification of your product is most important at this stage. Questions to be answered include the following:

- How extensively will you permit the product to be modified to include additions, ranges, colour selection, custom selection by the client, packaging, distribution, and future development of a complimentary range, all affecting the pricing structure? A downturn in sales will frequently encourage your salespersons to recommend and justify a modification of product. Be aware that any modification may result in redundancies and lost income.

- Additions: Is the product adaptable to additional facilities or services, all related or connected to the original?
- Ranges: Is the extension of the product to a wider range practical and desirable, being aware that an extension of ranges may be essential to retain client interest? This may be an aspect for future development, thus giving the impression of annual improvements. Regular improvements are always readily accepted by the market as an indication of a reputable company.
- Colour selection: The client will always want a wider range of colours. Care and strength in control is necessary to determine a practical and controllable range and to resist wide variation from the established range. There will always be good reasons to extend a range of colours, especially from salespersons and clients. The argument will be that such an extension will improve sales. Rarely is this the case, and trying to satisfy these requests will result in an uncontrollable, unwieldy, and expensive range of colours, resulting in expensive redundant stocks of product and raw material. This all means lost profit.
- Custom selection: If not rigidly controlled, the client will frequently ask for product additions, design changes, and other non-standard aspects. Unless procedures are specifically created to control custom design and production, exercise care as variation inspecification can lead to quality and cost-control disasters.
- Packaging: What packaging will you provide for the product? Here, again, costs can become prohibitive if design and decoration are not controlled. Package design and standardisation, colour minimisation, cost of supply, environmental concerns, and cost of production may all be areas of requested change. Remember, however, that packaging design and colour is a major aspect of marketing and impulse buying.

- Distribution: How extensive will the area of distribution be involved? Transport over long distances can be expensive and difficult to control. Movement and handling will create its own problems for product protection and packaging selection. Distance involves longer lead times for client supply, and client satisfaction is always more difficult from a distance. It may be that you need to consider agencies or franchises to cater for distance supply. They, in turn, could be encouraged to hold a minimum supply of stock in order to satisfy client's urgent requirements.

- Product range: The wider the range of product, the more costly is production. However, it may be necessary to create a range, albeit limited, to provide an all-round service to the client at large. There are many instances in the marketplace where businesses have commenced with a restricted range, gradually extending the range, as client acceptance developed and knowledge of the client's requirements were recognised. However, slow reaction to this subject may encourage competitors to infiltrate and provide this diversification at the expense of your sales. If yours is a professional practice, you may decide to expand the product range to include associated services that are traditionally provided by a separate professional. The inclusion of the extended range may attract customers and enhance your market penetration.

- Pricing of range: The pricing of the range of products is necessary at this early stage as it will affect your decisions regarding the final product you plan to provide. Client acceptance of your product will largely depend upon the type of client you will attract. If you plan to supply to a lower economic community, you will need to keep your pricing within an acceptable range. Alternatively, if the client is not so majorly influenced by price, this will not be such a concerning factor. Factors affecting this will also include wholesale distributorship, franchise demands, direct client supply, and your expected profit margin. All these aspects will eventually be documented into the financial planning section.

You should now have decided on the product and/or service you will provide and the related aspects described in this section. Your final decisions should now be documented for future inclusion into the Strategic Plan. You will not remember, so write them down.

The following example is an indication of product-planning documentation, which should be written into your final Strategic Plan.

Product Identification (1st Year)	Product Range (5 Years)	Distribution (1st Year)	Distribution (5 Years)
Document product/service identification. Limit identification to initial twelve months' operation.	Identify your decision regarding expansion of the product range over ensuing five years.	Document your decision regarding the extent of distribution over the first twelve months.	Identify your decision and document regarding the expansion of the geographical area of distribution over the ensuing five years.
Custom Product Selection	**Colour Selection**	**Packaging**	**Pricing**
Document your decision regarding the control over design and future fragmentation to conform to client's requests.	Document your decision regarding colour of product and the intention to control the diversification of colours.	Document your decision regarding packaging design, product protection, colour, and decoration.	Document your estimation of product/service price regarding community acceptance. This may change following your detailed costing.

It is essential to document your decisions for future reference and/or modification. You will not remember later. Establish a folder, electronically or manually, in which you can file all these decision-making elements.

CHAPTER 6

BUSINESS LOCATION

Depending on the type of business you have selected, you will need to consider the location from which you will operate. It may be that the business is already established, and this subject of location is fixed, albeit temporarily. There are several aspects for consideration, and they are as follows:

- If it is an established business, you need to consider the following aspects:
1. Relocation, as the present position may not comply with your Vision. It may be that the present position does not allow for expansion. On the other hand, it may be too expansive for your envisaged reduced activity levels.
2. Alternatively, the present position may be too large and not suitable for your vision, or it may not be ideal from a marketing viewpoint.

- You will need to consider whether your business is to be a service, professional, retail, health or food related, manufacturing, construction or other discipline:
1. Use of your personal residence. This is the less expensive option, but it is fraught with danger as you can quickly become a victim of your environment, never having an opportunity to relax and get away from the pressures, frustration, and stress of the business. This can create, in the client's mind, a

less expensive experience but may also convey a perception of amateurish and non-professional activity. It is essential to convey professionalism.

2. Rent or buy a suitable building or section of a building. Consider the option of renting a situation to begin, until you determine your exact requirements. You can relocate at a future time. Serviced office accommodation can be an attractive proposition, where reception, cleaning, and perhaps other services are provided.

3. Consider the need to provide for access to main highways. Transport can be a major problem if ready access is difficult. Access to main highways, rail freight spurs, airways freight facilities, and harbour shipping wharves should all be considered and taken on board or rejected.

4. Proximity to similar businesses: Fast-food outlets tend to congregate together as marketing philosophies demand that nearness to other similar food outlets creates successful public attraction. Consider the example of Kentucky Fried Chicken, McDonald's, and Happy Jacks. Frequently, they are located close to each other.

5. Consider the availability of professional, skilled, and unskilled employees and the public transport resources that are available. This is a major factor for the success of your business. Readily available employees, who can attend their employment without transport difficulties, will allay future employee problems and, if possible, union-oriented demands for travel allowances or increased remuneration. There are many examples where large manufacturing companies have successfully relocated large distances to relieve employee-related problems.

6. The density of passing traffic or pedestrian intensity can be a marketing influence. For some situations such as dentistry, optician, and the like, you may be better suited to shopping malls or in proximity to such. Alternatively, the business may

benefit by being situated on high-density highways where ready street advertising can be applied.

As your decisions are determined, document them and place them into a folder for inclusion into the Strategic Plan folder for future reference at a later time.

CHAPTER 7

COUNCIL/GOVERNMENTAL APPROVALS

Depending on where you are located and what governmental regulations control your product, service, location, or industry/business and whether they may be local, state, or federal or other, they all must be considered. There is always a temptation to ignore the regulations and the related costs involved or to consider that any regulations do not necessarily apply to you. However, be aware that you will eventually be caught out and may be subject to disastrous effects. Government inspectors can be increasingly difficult and intrusive if they believe you are endeavouring to avoid regulations. There are many examples of disastrous demands by governments at all levels which, if the basic and initial requirements were responsibly researched and applied on time by the business owner, they would have been avoided. Indeed, governmental advice, at all levels, can be available and heeded with resultant cost savings and business advantages, provided that, and if, you first create a perception of professional responsibility.

Some of these legislative requirements can be utilised as marketing aids. Items such as industry registration will give the impression of professionalism. Or similarly, registered premises would provide a perception of reliability.

If your plans include operations in another state, county, or even country, it may be strategic to establish an office in that location and also apply any local governmental requirements to that location, thus providing proof of location, which can be used as an advantage where contracts may be restricted to local citizens.

CHAPTER 8

STRATEGIC PLAN

8.1 Vision

You would have, by now, decided on your product and would be having a reasonable idea about your intended business activities. This next section can be most exciting, so leave your negative thoughts behind, polish your looking glass, gather as much local knowledge and research as you reasonably can, and be prepared to look into your future.

Now, put on your thinking cap and create your business 'Vision' for the ensuing five years. The best way to determine this, from my experience, is to conduct a brainstorming session with your close associates (all must be positive thinkers), or by yourself in isolation, although this can be biased and restricted. Pick a time and place where there will be no interruptions. Quite often, depending on expense constraints, a weekend away in a holiday location with the selected participants can be beneficial. This can permit complete concentration on the planning exercise and can be conducted in a disciplined situation without interruption. It seems to be that the most advantageous group of participants in this exercise would include some associates closely allied to the business, close reliable friends who have exhibited business acumen, reliable business associates, and the external accountant, should you have employed such a person.

I have often used the 'herringbone' diagram for this exercise. A herringbone diagram should be depicted on a large sheet of paper or a suitable large whiteboard, which can be displayed in a prominent position. The diagram should consist of a central horizontal line pointing towards a 'Vision' yet to be created. From this horizontal line, addendums should be drawn off such as shooting lines as in a herringbone skeleton. Each of these offshoots should represent and be titled for inclusion into the final Vision. These major titled branches should be predetermined by you. Attached to these branches will be leg stickers, containing suggestions for the Vision relative to the major branch to which it is adhered. All interested and involved persons should be encouraged to enter their thoughts on to the diagram as leg stickers. Each sticker should carry a summarised description of the suggested 'Vision' (refer following example). Following an appropriate elapsed time, remove all the leg stickers and record them in a section relative to the major leg from which they are removed. Repeat this for each major leg. You should now have several sections matching the major branches recorded on the herringbone diagram, each section with the many statements that were attached to the major branch.

Review and analyse each major section by title and by each minor entry. Discard and include as appropriate in accord with that which reflects, accurately, your Vision.

Finally, you will be left with a skeletal assembly of section subjects and related statements, all of which, when combined into a simple statement, will provide a draft of your Vision.

Herringbone example used for the Strategic Plan/Vision development

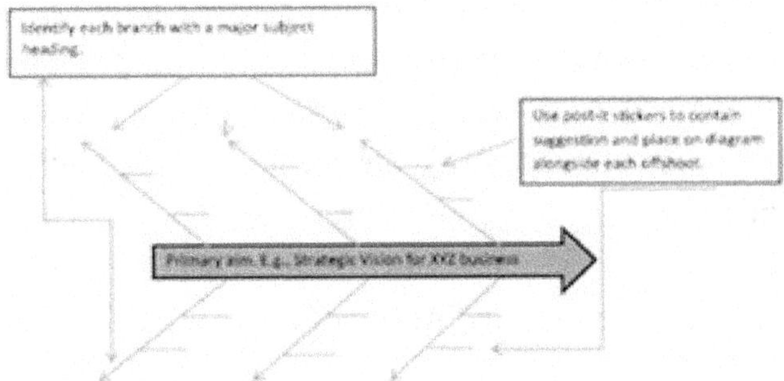

If the Vision is to be developed during a weekend away, the Herringbone concept may be developed, applied, and discussed in detail, whilst at the conference. Otherwise the Herringbone could be developed over several days or even weeks and then discussed, finalised, during the referred week end.

The 'Vision' must be clear and achievable. This Vision described in a short statement will, and must, guide every business decision made by you and your staff. Every business decision made during the daily and long-term operations of the business must have a 'direction' towards the eventual achievement of this strategic 'Vision'. Any plans and/or decisions that do not fit these criteria must be removed or ignored unless the overall vision is modified to include an avenue for the new or revised plan. However, this is fraught with danger, and considerable thought must be given before any change to the original vision is applied.

Banks, future financial partners, and business associates will be particularly interested, and encouraged, by your documented 'Vision'. Clients and business associates will be guided and enthused by an ambitious, achievable, short, and impressive 'Vision'.

The documented 'Vision', once satisfactorily completed, should be displayed in a prominent position within your business area. It should be included in all important outgoing policy documentation. It should become the centreboard for all business decision-making.

Remember, the 'Vision' should be ambitious, achievable, positive, clear, and logical. Indeed, on rare occasions, it may be that you want the business to remain stable, without development, or even to reduce in size or diminish the existing distribution area. Such desires are inherent with risk and should be given much thought before any final decision is decided. At the end of the day, when the final decision is made, this should be reflected in the documented 'Vision'.

Due to the recommended extensive distribution of the Vision, it should, therefore, not include confidential or delicate business information.

- As a few examples, the following may guide you in the creation of the business Vision:
- 'The XYZ company will service the Central Business District with excellence of product (service), providing supreme quality of product and client service, developing by the year 2020, sufficient in capacity to encompass the entire national distribution network'.
- 'The XYZ business, established in the year 2014, will provide excellent quality, timely service, and client support, becoming the leaders in its particular field of operation by the year 2020'.

'The XYZ Company plans to increase the quality of service and effectiveness of their product, whilst reducing the area of service and client strength, to a position of professional leadership in a smaller although intense situation by the year 2020'.

The development of this 'Vision' statement has been an essential activity, and its importance cannot be sufficiently emphasised, as it will direct the path and decision-making process for you and your staff for the ensuing five years and until a revised 'Vision' is created and distributed. The temptation to embark on a diverse direction, alien to the Vision concept, should be resisted at all costs, unless firstly, the Vision is amended to allow for this change in direction.

Write down your final 'Vision' for use in the Strategic Plan during the appropriate time of the overall business development…

8.2 Mission Statement

Contrary to the fact that the Strategic Vision has been developed to guide the path of the business for the ensuing five years, the Mission Statement should be concise, detailed, and structured to direct the business direction for the imminent twelve months. It should relate to the Vision and detail activities that will achieve the Vision direction. It should, of necessity, be more verbose and detailed, although retaining a simple concise logic. It should consist of several statements, each directed towards a specific goal to be achieved within the twelve months. These statements, therefore, should be measurable, reportable, and communicative to all staff, where applicable, and, importantly, restricted in distribution to those with whom confidentiality is assured.

The Mission Statement should relate responsibilities by name and lead to action items for inclusion into 'Action Sheets', to be explained later, for the execution of tasks, as detailed throughout the Mission Statement. This affords ready and regular audit, correction, amendment, and management direction, leading to successful achievement of the Mission Statement and, therefore, the planned positive development of the business.

The Mission Statement should be documented, as with the Vision, and should be published, displayed, and distributed to all internal and involved associates. However, it may demand, of necessity in part, confidentiality and, as such, should be secured from external parties. Additionally, and perhaps alternatively, confidentiality can be maintained through exclusion of sensitive information from the published information.

Example Mission Statement

'The XYZ company will, over the ensuing twelve months, expand its business activities in order to encompass the outer areas of the ABC country. It will create improved customer recognition of quality and excellence of product/service. It will achieve a 10% increase in sales volume across all products and, through a planned exercise of productivity, reduce operating costs by 5%. All operating decisions will be directed towards the achievement of this plan'.

'The XYZ business will provide excellence of service and customer satisfaction during the foregoing twelve months. It will be conscious of the need to reduce expense in order to provide an economic service and product to the immediate community. The prices set for the products will be reduced by 5% and carry with it a respective reduction in the cost of supply. The profitability of the organisation will be increased to 18% of Sales throughout, through a reduction in overhead expense, a strict control of suppliers costing, and the aforementioned sales pricing adjustment, thus producing an increased Sales volume.

Having determined your final Vision and Mission statements, all future business decisions mustbe made by you and your designated staff in accordance with these statements. Thus, the direction of your everyday operations must not vary from your goal for successful development. Any variation that may cause a fragmentation of effort and coordination can always be traced to activities and/or decisions that are not in accordance with your policies reflected in the two statements.

Of course, the Vision and Mission statements can be amended as circumstances change, or your own desires demand a varied direction. However, any amendment must be done with care and only after in-depth consideration and research and must be suitably and formally documented, communicated, and distributed to all concerned, including all who received the original documented statements.

All development and planning of this Business Plan will be influenced and directed by the Statements you have created.

8.3 Marketing

All businesses, regardless of the discipline, need an initial and an ongoing, marketing plan. Customers do not idly approach you or your business without some form of introduction, an interest in your product or service, or through your exposure to the community. However, all marketing is an expense and, often, cannot be justified economically. Many inexperienced business people mistakenly ignore marketing activities in the justification of expense saving and, therefore, additional profits. They believe that expense saved from marketing will increase the profit line accordingly. This is not necessarily correct. Marketing, to the uninitiated, can be frustrating, stressful, and without real meaning. This is a mistake. Marketing activity is essential at all levels and needs to occur continuously, regardless of how successful you and your business may become. Successful businesses have collapsed overnight purely because they have ignored the simplest of marketing requirements. However, neither should marketing be conducted without any thought to prudent economics. Each step must be researched and evaluated. Marketing must be planned, executed, measured, and amended where necessary. It is a continuous process, and what may be effective now may not be so effective tomorrow. Initial marketing strategies are rarely effective as ongoing policies and, therefore, may require amendment or a change of policy as the business prosperity or success occurs.

Word-of-mouth referral is most effective but difficult to achieve. Be aware that bad news travels like lightning, and is usually exaggerated, while good news is usually of no one's interest. Think of the person who buys a sandwich from the corner store. The first bite reveals that it consists of something bad and unpalatable. Irrespective of whether the sandwich is replaced free of charge or not, the offended person will happily repeat, and perhaps exaggerate, this experience to all and sundry. They, in turn, are just as zealous in passing on the bad news. And so the reputation of the shop is damaged very quickly, often irreparably. Now, another person buys a sandwich that is perfect in every way, even to the extent of exceeding the buyer's expectations. This is rarely passed on. Who wants to know? Perhaps, in the future, one might mention that they bought a nice sandwich from the shop, but never is this observation passed on as quickly as the former, nor with such seeming delight.

Initially, marketing activities need not be expensive. Letter drops, telephone solicitation, news media, personal cold-calling, personal interviews, and solicitation with key influential figures are all factors for consideration. Support and recommendation from community leaders can be effective. Introduction gifts and free lotteries with inexpensive prizes can contribute. Media exposure, in the form of news items of interest, can be effective marketing tools. On occasions, an opportunity may arise to couple marketing activities with another associated business. This can sometimes prove beneficial. However, exercise care as equally, it can prove to be only supporting another's activities.

Marketing must be designed to achieve a desired outcome. Ask yourself what is required from the marketing activity, and design your planned activity around your honest answer. Measure the cost and expected return. Most small business marketing activity can be planned and executed by the proprietor, and there is no need for specialist professional contractors or staff. As the business grows, it may be that there is a need for professional assistance, but exercise caution as this can cost excessive, wasteful dollars.

You may be inundated by salespersons selling all forms of marketing activities. Be careful in your selection. These salespersons will not accept any responsibility for failure, and it will be your cash at stake. You should thoroughly research each and every offer and suggestion, and do not be fearful of saying 'no'. Always bargain for a better deal, before accepting an offer of an advertising service.

Consider the type of penetration.

- Industry awareness.
  Individual approach to business leaders and other business management will prove beneficial. Direct your approach to the highest level. It may be that your endeavours are directed towards a person who has an alliance with your competitors, and you will have wasted your time. Similarly, direct mail, personal interviews, industry meetings, networking through associations, inclusion on tender and contract requests, and solicitation of work from larger like businesses. This latter method is often applied as it can be both beneficial to the larger business and yourself. If related to the building and construction industries, meetings with architects and governmental agencies are essential avenues for inclusion on tender requests.

- Professional services.
  Create community awareness through letter drops and networking through organisation memberships. Your regular attendance at industry meetings and social gatherings of professional groups is a necessary avenue for contacts. The catch phrase for this type of community awareness is 'networking', and it is essential that you allocate your time,

usually after hours, to this medium. Pass out plenty of your business cards. Pay attention to the design of your cards as they are a continuing reminder to the carrier that you can provide their requirements. These cards are inexpensive and often return business.

- Retail and food.
  Letter drops, local radio interviews, support and recommendation from community leaders, special one-off situations that may create opportunities, and many more individually presented awareness activities. At the start-up of your small retail business, consider free lotteries for clients with small gifts as prizes. All of these are relevant. However, the most effective method of promotion and advertising is in your manner and efficiency of service and client recognition. Bad news spreads like wildfire. Good news takes longer. Remember the sandwich example?

- Television and radio.
  Be aware of the cost and potential return of these mediums. They can be effective and relatively inexpensive, however, alternatively they can be equally expensive and ineffective. So apply caution. And particularly, before commitment, all avenues must be researched thoroughly for effectiveness and applied frugally.

- Web pages, Facebook, Twitter, and all other electronic medium are worth considering in the light of your business identity. However, exercise care. Not all potential customers are familiar with modern methods of Intelligence Transfer. Be aware that statements placed in the media can be international, can be usurped, and may be difficult to remove. Finally, document your marketing plans, applying timely dates and relevant costs.

8.4 Product Cost/Pricing/Margins

Create a listing of product/service costs as shown in the following. This will be the beginning of determining your sales pricing and your Profit and Loss Account details. It is surprising that many business owners do not know the accurate cost of their product or service. They incorrectly believe that the resultant Profit or Loss will determine whether the selling prices are accurate or need adjusting. This is incorrect and is another valid reason for eventual business disaster.

It may be that professional services and other selected areas may be price-controlled. This analysis is still required. **Product cost per 100 complete items (products or services)**

Cost in dollars per 100 items

Product	Product, Purchase Cost	Parts, Product, Manufacture	Direct Labour	Total Per 100 Items Cost	Overhead	Total Cost Per 100 Items, Including Overhead
Include all products in the product range. Include all services if yours is a service organisation.	Individual component or complete product purchase cost as some complete product may be purchased externally.	In-house manufacture, material, machine costs, and other direct costings.	Labour attributable to actual in-house manufacture	Using the foregoing, calculate the total cost of the product and/or service for 100 items.	Consists of all indirect expenses, including non-productive labour, power, property rent, and all expense that is not connected to actual product or service creation. At this stage, without any detailed knowledge, assume that overhead comprises 100% of total product cost.	Combine total cost of 100 product/service with overhead
Product 1	500	1,000	100	1,600	1,600	3,200
Product 2	750	300	50	1,100	1,100	2,200
Product 3	1,000	nil	nil	1,000	1,000	2,000
Service 1	nil	nil		6,000	6,000	12,000

This product/service costing analysis will provide for all the costs of your business, including product/service and overheads. Note that the direct purchase of goods, services, componentry, in-house manufacturing, labour costs, and overheads have all been included in the costing. These costs will play a major part in your financial control of the business. The actual costs should be controlled to reflect comparison and conformity with these figures, or amendments must be necessarily applied. That is, during manufacture or service, ensure that the actual costs of operating the business conform to these figures, or else, amend the operation/actual cost, or the predetermined figures, ensuring that actual and forecast figures match.

Product pricing

The costing conducted thus far only allows for the cost of operations and product provision, whether that is from external sources or from within. Providing the business operates perfectly as you have thus far estimated, all the estimated profit must come from the margin you are about to calculate. I have estimated for a 15% profit margin as seen in the following Finance Budget. That is 15% of Sales $. Therefore, you must add 20% to the product total cost, which includes overheads, to arrive at the selling cost. This percentage is approximate and should be varied, following actual results, in order to achieve the planned 15%. At all times, though, be perceptive of the market reactions, and apply variation to this figure, depending on that which you perceive will be acceptable in the market. It may be that you can achieve a higher profit return by applying a higher percentage, but be careful.

Selling prices, therefore, for the four items in dollars are as follows:

	Total Cost Plus Overhead Per 100	Margin Required Plus 20%	Total Selling Price Per 100 Items
Product 1	3,200	640	3,840
Product 2	2,200	440	2,640
Product 3	2,000	400	2,400
Service 1	12,000	2,400	14,400

These prices of cost, overheads, and total selling price will be included in the financial budgets to be developed later. It is important at this stage that the costs are reasonably accurate. Therefore, supplier's pricing (albeit probably estimated by the supplier at this stage), staff numbers, and financial wages, expenses etc. (particularly that for direct manufacture and service) are necessary in order to determine effective estimates. Wages that will be incurred within your business (other than direct wages/labour) and expenses incurred to operate your business are included in the overhead allowance.

At this stage, you will be in a position to reconsider the selling prices that you have already estimated. It may be that you believe the market or your competitors' prices will permit increases over those you have already determined. It is, therefore, advisable at this stage to document these amendments by adding another column for 'market price'. However, if the market or the competitors are selling for less than your determined prices, it would be unwise to create any reduction in your determined prices at this stage. Rather, delay any decision regarding reductions until the Financial Budgets are completed.

Revised selling prices as a result of market identification

	Total Cost Plus Overhead Per 100	Margin Required Plus 20%	Total Selling Price Per 100 Items	Market Perception of Price Per 100 Items
Product 1	3,200	640	3,840	3,840 (no change)
Product 2	2,200	440	2,640	3,200 (note increase)
Product 3	2,000	400	2,400	3,000 (note increase)
Service 1	12,000	2,400	14,400	14,400 (no increase)

8.5 Facilities and Equipment

This subject requires three separate sections. First, the equipment and facilities you will require at the commencement of your operation, secondly, the additional equipment and facilities you will require after six months of trading, and thirdly, the additional equipment and facilities you will require after the first twelve months.

Consider the purchase of second-hand items as these are often sufficiently effective with which to commence and will be substantially less expensive.

Office facilities in good condition can often be acquired from auction houses at a fraction of the new purchase price. Computers need not be the more expensive to start. Manufacturing equipment can similarly be acquired for low prices from many 'used' equipment sources. Professional and other selected situations may need new and proven equipment, but care must be exercised in responsible selection.

Watch out for sales of equipment from disabled companies as often the prices of this equipment are very low and this can conserve much expense.

At this stage, however, merely determine what is required for each of the three stages. Availability and pricing can be investigated at a later time. It is sufficient to apply an estimate of the cost of each item for the Strategic Plan Financial Pricing. This pricing will represent a **Capital Expenditure Budget.**

CHAPTER 9

SALES BUDGET

Now, you are nearly there. Keep the crystal ball polished. You have to now forecast the numbers of each product you will sell in each period—in the case of this guide, quarterly. This, incidentally, is the maximum period you should consider. Ideally, monthly would be a safer planning situation; however, you must consider the personal time involved in maintaining a shorter period, and your primary aim should be to keep it simple. As the business is about to start, the estimates should commence low and increase as you become successful. Of course, later on, there may be occasions when, through circumstances, you might decide to reduce the quantities for some specific reason. And, of course, the more often you forecast, and the more historical data to which you will have access, the more accurate your forecasts will be.

I have been told many times by senior management and hard-nosed business owners, to whom I may have been consulting, that no one can say what their activity will be in the future. They strived to convince me that it is impossible to plan activity levels ahead with any accuracy. This opinion is not correct. The more often forecasting is carried out, using all the forecasting factors available, the more accurate those forecasts will become. An example of relevant factors is—

- state and world economic conditions
- climatic conditions

- seasonal factors
- past sales experience
- historical factors
- your own expectations

You must estimate. Any figure is better than none, and your estimates will be self-correcting as the period of estimation progresses.

Competitive activity: Although it is your responsibility to ensure you are sufficiently active and innovative to keep ahead of competitors, what they do should not overly concern you. Continual and incessant peering into your competitors' activities will impede the performance and innovative progression of your own business. Let your competitors be aware of your activities, and let them do the worrying. Of course, you must be aware of their activities, but keep them in your rear-view mirror! Time spent on the detailed analysis of your competitors' activities will impede your own progress.

Sales budget by quarter in AUD $

The foregoing unit totals have been applied against the total prices per hundred units, using the revised increased selling prices, considering market perceptions.

Item	Quart 1	Quart 2	Quart 3	Quart 4	Annual Total
Product 1	7,680	15,360	23,040	42,240	88,320
Product 2	3,960	7,920	21,120	23,760	56,760
Product 3	6,000	13,200	16,800	21,600	57,600
Service 1	7,200	14,400	36,000	59,600	117,200
Total AUD $	24,840	50,880	96,960	147,200	319,880 say (320,000)

Note that the total of $319,880 has been rounded up to $320,000 for simplicity of future calculations. This sales budget schedule should be maintained with an additional column at each quarterly section to show quarterly actual performances. Variances should be immediately addressed, and either corrected to show a realistic estimate for the future, or create some amendment to your operation to obtain a correction in the sales. The sales budget figures shown are the sales figures to be included in the Financial Budget.

CHAPTER 10
PRODUCTION BUDGET

Following the previous planning exercises, wherein the direction and validity of the business was determined, you are now in a position to begin the planning and preparation tasks for the manufacture and acquisition of the product range. For those businesses planning to manufacture, it is necessary to plan a 'make' budget and those planning to sell purchased product only to plan a 'buy' or 'purchasing' budget. A manufacturing facility will usually demand a 'buy' and a 'make' situation. In order to ensure that product is available for delivery to clients on time, it is necessary that those products are in stock or are being manufactured according to a committed delivery schedule, acceptable to the client. Similarly, purchased product must also be received into store in time for the scheduled use by manufacturing or in readiness for delivery to the client. Alternatively, determine that if a regularly provided product is required either for manufacturing or for supply as a finished product to the client, it is received into store in time to supplement stock in accordance with a predetermined and approved stock level. Therefore, this will mean purchased product, componentry, raw material, and packaging is ordered in sufficient time to ensure it is available for assembly, manufacture, and delivery as demanded by the required sales scheduled timing.

Larger and established businesses, involved in manufacture and procurement of finished product, usually can access a pre-designed computer program which accommodates all these planning requirements. Unfortunately, too many operatives use these programs without the basic knowledge of manufacturing planning principles, often with disastrous results. Small business, such as the one you are contemplating creating, should initially disregard the custom computer programs and plan manually, thus providing a detailed knowledge of the methods and principles used to determine adequate supply and the ability to be personally familiar with every aspect of the supply procedure. Additionally, computer programs for small manufacturing businesses, irrespective of assurances to the contrary, are expensive in procurement, set-up, training, continual 'essential' upgrade, with resultant and frequent errors and problems being readily blamed on the 'computer'. Shop floor personnel such as supervision and, perhaps, after-hours or shift personnel, unless they are computer literate, are at a loss to solve planning problems or interpret planning situations without reference to readily available advisors. Perhaps programs are more at risk if the personnel are somewhat computer-literate and are tempted to change programs without intimate knowledge of the consequences of their actions. Therefore, I suggest throughout all your initial business planning explained in this text, you steer clear of custom computer programs and restrict your activity to simple computer spreadsheet or manual compilation. You may progress to pre-designed computer programs at a later stage when you are sufficiently familiar with the process that you will identify when strange or incorrect figures are produced by the program. Be aware, however, that those computer errors are invariably the result of human input errors. And the latter seem to occur with monotonous regularity.

10.1 Procurement

First, identify all the products, components, raw material, and packaging required to provide for the sales budget. Create a file for each item, and determine supplier lists, lead times, including your own manufacturing lead time, and quantities by period. In this guide, a quarterly period has been used. However, you can use any division you select, although I would not recommend anything longer than quarterly. In my own business, I always used monthly, which gave me more detailed, accurate, and timely advice. Record every item on to a master spreadsheet, allowing for lead times and quantities by period, separating procurement, and manufacturing lead times. Ensure and plan that raw material and purchased componentry is purchased and delivered in sufficient time to allow for lead times and manufacturing lead time. Establish prices, confirm lead times, and determine, through research and comparisons of price/delivery/ quality, a preferred supplier list.

Determine the cash and timing required for procurement commitment, and retain this information for inclusion into the subsequent Cash Flow Analysis.

The unplanned will all too regularly occur, such as sales in excess of budget, late deliveries of procured items, in-house machine breakdowns, staff holidays, to mention a few. Therefore, it is wise to maintain a stock level, albeit minimal. Remember, excess stock is costly, so keep it to an absolute minimum which will mean a balanced situation, and you will not always be right. When stock-outs occur, the temptation will be to hold a larger stockholding. Be careful, and if this is necessary, again, keep the extra stock to a minimum. A discontinued product or a change of specification to align with the client's desires can mean obsolete stock and, therefore, financial loss. An occasional stock-out is preferable to a larger stockholding. It can also be a temptation to avail oneself of special offers, seemingly at reduced cost, which will involve larger than normal orders. This is rarely a preferable exercise. The risk of costly, redundant, or outdated stock, coupled with the use of cash unnecessarily, far outweighs any savings in procurement.

So depending on the lead time of each procured item, add sufficient product of each intended item for procurement to match the delivery lead time of that item. Theoretically, this need only occur for the first time of ordering. Although, in practice, on each subsequent and regular ordering occasion, add or subtract any variation in the planned holding versus actual holding of stock at that time. Experience, after a time of operating, will determine more accurately what this stockholding should be.

You are now in readiness to commence procurement once the final decision to proceed with your business is established.

		Product Procurement Summary for Production						
	Supplier 1	Price per 100 AUD$	Supplier 2	Price per 100 AUD$	Preferred Supplier	1st Quarter require-ments	Lead time of pre-ferred Supplier	Date required
RM 1 kgs	XYZ Coy	600	Katies	580	KATIES	200	6 weeks	1st quar-ter - 1 month
RM2 met	ABC Coy	28	BNI	35	ABS Coy	350	2 months	1st quar-ter - 1 month
FP 1	Smith Coy	750	GHM	750	GHM	250	1 month	1st day 1st quarter
FP2	Roy Dod	1050	SAMS	1300	SAMS	500	2 months	1st Day 1st quarter
COMP1	ABC Coy	600	MAGS	550	MAGS	630	3 weeks	1st quar-ter - 1 month
COMP2	DEFE CIT	58	DES	49	DES	5000	1 month	1st quar-ter - 1 month
PACK 1	MAST DO	590	WRAP	590	MAST DO	780	3 months	1st quarter - 2 weeks
PACK 2		380	POMD	400	FOLD ME	1000	2 months	
	FOLD ME							1st quar-ter - 2 weeks

RM = Raw material

FP = Finished Product

COMP = Component

PACK = Packaging

Order Summary and Control for First Quarter. Note: Repeat Order Summary for each quarter or time period.

Item	Required	Units +/− Stock Variation	Total Units to Order	Cost Per 100 Units$	Total Cost of Order$	Preferred Supplier	Lead Time Weeks	Date to Order. Week Before Start Date	Order Priority and Done Yes/No
RM1	200	100	300	580	1,740	XYZ Coy	6	Start date minus 6 weeks	3
RM2	350	220	570	35	210	ABS Coy	8	Start date minus 8 weeks	2
FP1	250	80	330	750	2,250	GHM	4	Start date minus 4 weeks	4
FP2	500	340	840	1,300	10,900	SAMS	8	Start date minus 8 weeks	2
COMP1	630	160	990	550	5,500	MAGS	3	Start date minus 3 weeks	5
COMP2	5,000	1,650	6,650	49	320	DES	4	Start date minus 4 weeks	4
PACK 1	780	780	1,560	590	900	Mast Do	12	Start date minus 12 weeks	1
PACK 2	1,000	700	1,700	400	1,700	Fold Me	8	Start date minus 8 weeks	2
Total					23,520				

In this example, the priorities indicate that your ordering for each period should start with—

- Pack 1 from Must Do, 12 weeks before your planned start date for each quarter.
- RM2 from ABS Coy, 8 weeks before your planned start date for each quarter.
- FP2 from SAMS, 8 weeks before your planned start date for each quarter.
- AACK 2 from Fold Me, 8 weeks before your planned start date for each quarter.
- RM1 from XYZ Coy, 6 weeks before your planned start date for each quarter.
- FP1 from BHM, 4 weeks before your planned start date for each quarter.
- COMP2 from DES, 4 weeks before your planned start date for each quarter.
- COMP1 from MAGS, 3 weeks before your planned start date for each quarter.

This timing will apply to each quarter (period) and will only change should any of the lead times change, either extend or reduce so altering the order date accordingly.

You will recognise that your procurement must start well before the business commences and subsequently well before each following period.

Note that the Product Procurement Summary for Production is not related to previous tables and estimates. It is for demonstration purposes only. Similarly, the Order Summary and Control is based only on the Product Procurement for Production and has no relationship in detailed numbers to previous examples. Of course, you must balance all figures throughout your analyses to the same base.

The total cost of procurement, by period, should be included in the Cash Flow Analysis to be discussed later.

Stock has been included in the Order Summary and Control to ensure that variations in actual sales from budget can be accommodated without any serious adverse effect on the client's requirements. However, once the initial stockholding has been established, care should be exercised at all times to maintain this stock level at an absolute minimum. Adjustments at each time of ordering will ensure this occurs; otherwise, escalation in stockholding will utilise unnecessary funds, occupy excess space, and risk obsolete products when colours, design, and products are changed to fit with clients and the market's demands.

CHAPTER 11

OPERATIONS, SERVICE CENTRES, ACTIVITY

Naturally, the actual activity of your business will continually change, services will be reliant on the sometimes continually changing desires of the client, and your business innovation will be subject to ready changing circumstances. Be acceptable to change whilst always exercising caution.

11.1 Capacity Control

As the business develops, you will experience fluctuations in actual sales. I have discussed the occasions of downturns and non-achievement of sales budgets. However, there are times when the sales will unexpectedly and uncomfortably increase beyond the capacity of your manufacturing or service facility. On the surface, this appears to be a good aspect of your business, and it may be long-term. But in the short-term, it can be devastating through the many disadvantages of overcapacity and of being inundated with client's orders. Shortage of supplies to provide for unexpected increases in output, shortage of labour, insufficient time to provide may all be results of increased sales, all causing delays in delivery and subsequent client dissatisfaction. This can cause a long-term loss of client confidence and future loss of sales and business losses. Indeed, it has occurred that an undue increase in sales demand over the actual capacity of production, without sensible and considered adjustment, has caused an eventual dramatic loss of sales and subsequent business closure. This can be protected, and communication with your client always providing genuine estimates of late delivery are essential to secure and maintain client confidence.

Rapid replenishment of supplies even at a premium cost, increased labour (casual or temporary), additional equipment (purchased or hired), and temporary assistance by another manufacturer can all assist in overcoming a capacity shortage problem. You should be reasonably confident that an increased rate of sales will continue before committing to any ill-considered capacity- increase expense. In the short-term, an increase in the product pricing may slow down the sales intake while retaining, even increasing, the profit ratio of your business. In some circumstances, however, this can attract the reverse reaction in that, it may cause an increase in client perception of your business status and increase the sales yet further.

As mentioned earlier, in some circumstances, the advent of client orders can escalate unexpectedly and well beyond budgeted expectations. This, whilst appearing to be a good business outcome, can, if not controlled, be detrimental to the business and have long-term drastic consequences. For instance, an inability to supply can cause a long-term loss of clientele which may prove difficult, if not impossible, to recover. An unexpected increase in orders may cause rush situations in processing, resulting in a downturn in quality of product and/or service. Such a situation may also result in a similar loss of clientele. I have mentioned previously the possible control of excessive client orders through a price increase. Obviously, care must be exercised when using this strategy to ensure that the chance of losing clientele through high pricing is minimal and may only apply to new clients with whom the strategy is intended to apply. Conversely, the reverse can apply. A shortage of sales causing a non-achievement of budget can be rectified by adjusting the pricing downwards. Again, extreme care must be applied in these instances to ensure that the financial planning structure and fragmentation of the business is not dramatically and adversely affected. Idle, un-researched, and non-professionally determined price reductions are often made in the name of sales and marketing strategies, but unless you are aware of the calculated financial consequences, the result can ruin your business or at least create devastating financial crises.

Using a simple computer program, 'what if' examples of the Profit and Loss Statement can be readily created, indicating the situation results, should such variations in prices be applied.

11.2 Innovation

Innovation is a continual aspect of your business. It applies equally to Product and Service. It needs continual research and determination if that which you are providing your clients is acceptable and satisfactory with the changing times or if it needs improvement, upgrading, change, or replacement. Improvements in product design and in client's requirements, recognising when, through repeated client requests for differences, or stagnation in sales, or client enthusiasm are always at the forefront of your product-range variations and specifications. Similarly, improvements and economic upgrades should be continually considered, evaluating the quality, cost, and client reaction. Improved product, improved quality, and cost reduction can all readily be continually achieved through structured and considered product and manufacturing evaluation and change. Indeed, it is an established practice to regularly, say six monthly, to evaluate your products, endeavouring to study each component, reducing the cost of production (even design), whilst at the same time increasing the quality and client acceptability of the product.

In this manner, subjecting each product or component singly or individually to research, a Product and Service can best be addressed and advantageously assessed through a group situation. Group members need not necessarily be regularly involved with the business or the product in order to participate. An independent view can be both innovative and, at times, quite inventive. Each idea and suggestion should be considered for quality improvement, client usage improvement, cost reduction, and therefore, increased profit and environmental and safety enhancement.

The application of the Herringbone chart can be advantageous in attaining overall product improvement. It is a practical and simple way of harnessing group's suggestions and ideas and evaluating them in a logical manner which encourages quality decision-making.

This type of product enhancement should be a regular function, addressing, and readdressing, componentry and products on a rotational basis. Minimal improvement in quality and material savings can mean substantial increased sales and/or appreciable profit enhancement. Internal procedural analysis, in the same manner, can also mean enhanced client service and improved business activity, resulting in client satisfaction and increased profitability. All these enhancements can be equally applied to service organisations. Improvement and advancement in both product improvement and in productivity is never complete. It can always be improved with resultant profit improvement or at least stabilisation.

11.3 Staffing

Now that you have decided on a series of disciplines for your business, it is time to consider if, and to what extent, staffing will be required. Will it mean professional or qualified staff, or can you cope with untrained staff initially, subjecting them to your in-house training? Depending on your business activities, you may need qualified staff, but careful consideration is essential as qualifications demand increased salaries and, hence, added costing structures.

Conditions of employment will need to be established, being aware of the requirements of government legislation and any Union requirements that may be enforceable. Consider whether Unions will be involved or not. It is wise to determine your conditions of employment as close to the demands of your associated business conditions as economically possible, thus applying some internal protection against any unwarranted future external aggravation. However, if economically viable, it is sometimes wise and viable to apply Union requirements, even involving Union representatives in the determination and resultant staff conditions, in order to realise staff contentment and industrial peace. The inclusion of Union Representatives in this planning can have advantageous outcomes. Research the reputation of both the Union Representatives and any External Involvement first, for incorrect selection in any area can be disastrous and a waste of time.

However, this guide is essentially considering a small business, and therefore, staff numbers will be limited. The major aspects to consider are trust, ability, and compatibility. Always create simple staff contracts detail conditions of employment and have them signed by the new employees.

Consider salary levels, as these are required for inclusion into the financial analyses. However, it is a temptation to be overly generous, but be cautious and frugal. Once established it is difficult, even impossible to retract any offer.

11.4 External Consultants

Depending on your own abilities, consider the need for external consultancies. In some areas, irrespective of your own expertise, it is wise to employ external advice and assistance. The predominant assistance is usually business accountancy, to assist in both business advice and taxation annual returns. This assistance, if acquired early, and before the commencement of your business, will provide the advice and essential documentary assistance you will need in order to conform to governmental requirements. Care should be applied in the selection of an accountant, with cost estimates obtained, thus resulting in a reasonable expense for this service all of which will provide beneficial results throughout the growth of your business.

Such a service will usually divert intense governmental scrutiny as reputable business accountants are qualified and registered and subject themselves to rigorous credibility.

Another area of assistance may be the short-term engagement of a consultant to analyse the community reactions regarding the acceptance of your product or service. These results may prove valuable in the determination of your business advertising and general community activities. Again, this can be expensive and caution is advised.

And of course, depending on your own experience and expertise, you may require the considered assistance of an external person in other areas of dependency.

CHAPTER 12

FINANCIAL PLAN

There is now sufficient information to develop your Financial Plan, initially in the form of a Financial Budget. That is a basic Profit and Loss Statement.

Simple computer programs are available for this function, and when you commence your business, you should consider the purchase of one of these. However, it is essential that you understand the principles in the development of a Profit and Loss Statement as this will be an ongoing measurement of your business on a regular basis. It is, therefore, recommended that initially, the Financial Budget be created manually, perhaps assisted by a simple computer program. In this way, you will be able to specify detailed requirements for a tailored computer program later. Your regular review of this budget and its parameters, against the actual business performance, is essential in order to preserve profitable activity or, at least, to be immediately aware of unwarranted divergences from the envisaged, planned, business performance. I prefer this review to be conducted on a monthly basis although, as with the example shown herein, quarterly will suffice in the early stages of business activity. At this point, the exercise is to determine whether your intended business will be viable financially and this Profit and Loss Statement will provide that assurance or will clearly show where amendments in your estimations are necessary. It may even show that your business is not viable, and therefore, in this case, your efforts thus far have been invaluable in saving you from financial devastation, through entering into a potentially failing situation. I have known of instances where the embryo businessman has ignored the financial determination warnings, only to experience devastation in a very short period of time, resulting in bankruptcy.

Using a spreadsheet that may be computer-assisted or, preferably, manually determined, allocate columns to each of the periods you intend to measure, say quarterly at this stage. Provide a separate column alongside each allocation for the entry of subsequent 'actual' performances.

The spreadsheet rows should be identified by subject allocations as shown in the example. The rows should be divided into groups represented by—

Income, including subheadings such as Sales, Interest, and any other forms of business income.

Direct Costs, such as purchase of goods and services related directly to your product, and your business labour which will be, in turn, directly related to the creation of your product. A 'rule of thumb' estimate of Direct Costs for control purposes, although this depends largely on your type of business, is 40% of Income.

Gross Profit—This classification is the difference between the Income Total and the Direct Costs Total. As with Direct Costs in the foregoing, an estimate of Gross Profit for control purposes, although, again, this depends largely on your type of business, is 60% of Income.

Expenses, including subheadings for each and every type of expense which will be incurred by the business. Do not be concerned whether your classifications are subject to taxation or not, as your accountant will judge this at a future time. Your only concern at this stage is recording every expense incurred by the business, whatever the reason for that expense. Any expense notincluded will only subject the resultant profit figure to error and, perhaps, drastic review analyses. Again, as with Gross Profit, an estimation of Expenses can be in the order of 25% of Income. There is a practice among many accountants to exclude your own salary, or the proprietor's, from these expenses. These salaries, as with every other expense, must be included. Otherwise, there is no real understanding of the resultant profit.

Profit—The resultant entry of Profit is reflected in the difference between the Gross Profit and Expense totals. Depending largely on your type of business, 15% of Income is a common figure of attainment for a manufacturing business.

However, it must be stressed that these percentage estimates are only shown as examples, and the applicable estimates for your business can only be more accurately determined over a period of several terms of budget returns. They can be valuable and ready comparisons of business performance for your own analysis of your business operations, and for past trends and future estimates, of profitable activity.

At this stage, you may believe, as many business operators incorrectly believe, that you cannot foresee accurately what the future income and expense costs will be as these are dependent upon a plethora of external influences. This is not essentially correct. It is often surprising how accurate one can get with estimates. In any event, any figure is better than none, and experience over a period of time will correct any anomalies that may be estimated initially.

Estimating or budgeting is essential, and while it is recognised that you may not know what is going to happen in the future, there are many indicators that, when considered with your own knowledge, will provide a figure that can prove to be amazingly accurate. However, even if it is inaccurate, and although you will endeavour to reduce the resultant error as much as possible, it is a basis for comparison with 'actual' performance. Your estimates will, over time and subsequent budget revisions, become more accurate as you develop a history of performance, have a more intimate knowledge of the relevant external affectations, and establish a self- confidence of business success and expectation. Remember, as I often repeat, any figure is better than none, and after a somewhat short period of time, you will find that your forecasts are amazingly accurate.

The entry of data relative to your estimates should now be done. Consider each entry carefully. This includes the Income and in this case, the Sales and Cost of Sales. The Sales represent actual external customer service work done or product sold and delivered for that period. It does not include future orders. In this example, the Cost of Purchases relative to your product or service for each quarter has already been calculated, and this should be entered. The Total Cost of Sales subtracted from the Income will provide the Gross Profit for each period. Ideally, the Total Cost of Sales will compute to approximately 40% of Sales and the Gross Profit, therefore, 60% of Sales. Recall that this figure should be amended to reflect your own business results. If there is a marked variation from this, you must readdress the sales estimates and the cost of sales, endeavouring to amend your figures to provide the ideal margins specified. A falling short of these figures will inevitably drastically affect the Net Profit. This will be recognised as you proceed through this Financial Budgeting exercise.

Having listed every aspect of business expense that you will incur, you can now move into the expense area. Don't worry whether an entry is tax deductible. That will come later with your accountant. At this stage, list everything that will cause an expense. Even list your own spendingwhich, in your opinion, is attributable to the business and is not part of your own salary. Estimate the spending for each item for each period. Be as factual as possible, without exaggeration and without underestimating. Rationalisation of these entries will come later.

Determine the total expense. This should equal approximately 45% of sales, subject to your own business activity.

Subtract the Expense total from the Gross Profit to provide for Net Profit, which should equate to approximately, and again relative to your own business, 15% of sales. You will now recognise that continual effort to achieve Gross Profit at 60% of sales (Direct Costs being 40%) and the Expense total at 45% of sales will protect your Net Profit of 15% of sales. The, Gross Profit, relies on the stability of purchasing prices of bought-in product, material and componentry, and if you include the direct labour attributable to the internal manufacture and creation of your product or service, Gross Profit also relies upon the efficiency of that labour and the material efficiency in your manufacturing section. So any reduction of these costs will increase the Gross Profit and, if all other are equal, will increase your Net Profit. Similarly, a reduction in Expenses will increase Net Profit if all other are equal. Of course, a short fall in sales will demand a commensurate reduction in both Cost of Sales and Expenses, and this is where expertise and experience in business acumen will prevail.

Having created the first attempt at the financial budget, the results might not bear any relationship to a viable business. The net profit might not give you any encouragement to press on. Don't be despondent, remembering that the figures used are only estimates. Work through every entry and endeavour to identify excesses whilst retaining a commitment to a factual performance. It may be that 'sales' could be genuinely increased without creating an impossible target. You may have been somewhat pessimistic in the initial estimate. Purchasing, Direct Labour, and Manufacturing Costs may have been excessively high, and a more realistic approach may provide a higher Gross Profit. As actual figures become available after the business has commenced, both these items will be self-correcting, although ongoing control is always essential. Direct labour inefficiency, material wastage through poor quality, and reject product and relaxation with suppliers and their prices will all increase the Cost of Sales and, therefore, reduce Gross Profit.

Expense Control is the most effective and immediate area for the reduction of costs. Expense is an area that does not return any income. It only uses cash without return, albeit necessarily, of course. So in this initial creation and in every future analysis, examine each and every item with a sensible yet 'Scrooge' mentality. Every dollar saved in this area directly improves the Net Profit. Ideally, the Net Profit should be 15% of the Sales volume, although, again, subject to your own business activity. It should never be less without a plausible, short-term reason if, and when, a reduction in expenses can be obtained so it will enhance Net Profit.

Finally, apply a tax encumbrance to the Net Profit to show the actual, final, free profit available to the business. This taxation estimate allowance should be retained as cash, whenever possible, in readiness for the advised taxation payment. Should the business results be such that sufficient cash is not available, a cumulative balance of taxation reserves should be recorded in order that when sufficient cash is available, the recorded cumulative total can be isolated. An engaged accountant will usually watch this aspect for you.

CHAPTER 13

FINANCIAL CONTROL

The following is a typical example of Profit and Loss Account. This is one of the most valuable control documents you will have. Every income and product cost and expense, whatever the cause, must be entered.

13.1 Profit and Loss Account

	Budgeted Profit and Loss Statement AUD $					
	1st Year of Operation					
	1st Quarter	2nd Quarter	3rd Quarter	4th Quarter	Total	
Income						
Sales						
Product 1	7,680	15,360	23,040	42,240	88,320	
Product 2	3,960	7,920	21,120	23,760	56,760	
Product 3	6,000	13,200	16,800	21,600	57,600	
Service 1	7,200	14,400	36,000	59,600	117,200	
Total	24,840	50,880	96,960	147,200	**319,880**	
Cost of Sales						

Purchased Product	4,625	9,750	16,000	21,250	51,625	
Direct Labour Manufacturing/ Service	5,725	11,450	24,400	39,250	80,825	
Subtotal	10,350	21,200	40,400	60,500	**132,450**	41% of sales
Gross Profit	14,490	29,680	56,560	86,700	**187,430**	59% of sales
Expenses						
Accountant		300		600	900	
Advertising	90	0	50	60	200	
Bank Charges	50	50	50	50	200	
Car Expenses						
Fuel	60	50	50	40	200	
Insurance	700				700	
Licence	150				150	
Registration	600				600	
Repairs		60	120	420	600	
Service		150	150	200	500	
Computers	100		250	150	500	
Govt. Charges		120		180	300	
Innovation		100		100	200	
Insurance	800				800	
Mail	120	60	60	60	300	
Power	200	180	180	140	700	
Rental	1,375	1,375	1,375	1,375	5,500	
Security	110	110	110	110	440	
Stationary	100	60	60	60	280	
Telephone	100	100	100	150	450	
Wages						
Self	17,600	17,600	17,600	17,600	70,400	
Staff	15,000	15,000	15,000	15,000	60,000	

Total	37,155	35,315	35,155	36,295	**143,920**	45% of sales
Net Profit	−22,665	−5635	21,405	50,405	**43,510**	14% of sales
Tax prov. 30%					13,053	
NP after Tax					30,457	
	Summary COS = 41% of Sales Gross Profit = 59% of Sales Expenses/Overheads = 45% of Sales Net Profit = 14% of Sales					
These percentages provide a valuable 'rule of thumb' estimating tool for determining prices and approximate profit.						

Control of your business viability, reflecting operating results for a designated period, is acontinuing exercise and mainly initiated using this Profit and Loss Statement as a base and knowledge source. Never underestimate the importance of this document. By examining the Profit and Loss figures each period, and addressing any predominant and serious variation, you will ensure a control that will provide you with a timely knowledge, thus making you aware of the opportunity to correct any happening that jeopardises the continuing health of your business. Often, and hopefully more often than not, the Profit Budget will be achieved or even exceeded. Great, but where is the money? The calculated actual profit, using actual operating results, should be identifiable and reflected through the available cash. But if the cash is not present, and it mostly is not evident, then you must search for reasons and/or excesses in the operative areas that will use cash excessively or unnecessarily. Therefore, you must quickly analyse the outstanding debtors or any prepaid creditors or overstocking or any area of outgoing or withheld cash within the accounts of both the Profit and Loss Statement and the Balance Sheet. The Profit and Loss Statement will indicate all operating variances over a given period, and the Balance Sheet will accurately show the financial situation of the business at a selected point in time. This will be explained in detail later in this text. Hence, providing you have maintained your operating records current, then a Balance Sheet can be created at any time, and this will reflect the state of the business at that time. Another interpretation of the Balance Sheet provides the knowledge of the extent of the Net Assets and Net Liabilities. These are shown on the Balance Sheet and provide an accurate knowledge of the situation should you close down your business, voluntarily or involuntarily, at that time. This is very important knowledge for you to have when making financial decisions regarding any aspect of your business going forward. Of course, excess cash that may be available, contrary to the Profit and Loss planning, must equally be subject to investigation and explanation, for a surplus of cash, without explanation, merely means that there is some miscalculation that will eventually, and probably at the most inopportune time, create an embarrassing business crisis of cash flow ineptitude.

Insufficient profit, or at less than that budgeted, may be identifiable in any of the following areas of the Profit and Loss Account.

13.2 Sales

A downward variation in sales will require effective and immediate correction. Determine areas of attention that will have a corrective effect and that will return sales to budget. Review your product range, particularly looking at those products and services that may be improved to return improved profits. You might consider inexpensive advertising programmes focused on specific areas such as letter drops, radio advertising, newspaper advertising, Internet exposure, and price reductions. Be aware that any price variation demands extreme caution and must initiate a careful and detailed review before any action is taken in this subject. In addition, address other areas of control to ensure that expenditure is reduced to conform to the reduced income. Study every Expense classification, striving to reduce expenditure in those areas.

13.3 Gross Profit

A less-than-budgeted result means that—

a) Sales are not as expected, and revision of budgets or aggressive remedial action may be required. This has been discussed. However if sales are returning budgeted results the following areas of control may require investigation.

b) Cost of sales may be higher than expected and may have been caused through—

a manufacturing direct labour, which is not efficient, and investigation into labour efficiencies may identify a weakness in manufacturing.

b material wastage, which may be occurring and which needs to be addressed. It may seem strange, but a regular sighting of the contents of the garbage bins may reveal a scrapping of material, through unrecorded manufacturing errors, resulting in reject material. It is surprising the number of occasions I discovered hidden mistakes in manufacturing, through rejected materials and componentry that had been discarded into the garbage bins, unrecorded.

c procurement costs which may have risen beyond reasonable budgeted expectations. Suppliers must be regularly controlled to obtain the continued best possible prices. In a small business, this would be your personal concern, but as you grow, you may employ the services of a specific supply clerk. Such an employee should be continually monitored to ensure the best supplier prices are obtained.

13.4 Expenses

This represents the overhead section of the business which should be maintained at the lowest, albeit sufficient, level of outgoing expenses. Higher than budgeted total expenses must immediately initiate a detailed investigation, item by item of the expense budget, in order to reduce this overhead section. Even during normal times when profit may be within budgeted parameters, a regular analysis of the expense items can be employed to reduce expenses and thus increase profit levels above the estimated 15%. Take each expense item at a time and examine why it is higher than expected and whether it can be reduced. Even if it is at a satisfactory level, a regular examination seeking a possible reduction is worthy of your time. Remarkably, expenses can quickly blow out of control without warning, unless they are strictly controlled. Your personal attention to this area is essential, irrespective of how large your business may grow. You will be surprised when, where, and how you can reduce expenditure merely through a simple inspection of practices. A reduction in Expenses relates to an equal increase in Profit. Every item of expense, regardless of how insignificant it is, is worthy of analysis.

13.5 Net Profit

The results of the financial analysis, explained in the foregoing, are revealed in the Net Profit section of that analysis. These results may be positive or negative. A negative result may be acceptable only during the initial development of your business and only where future forecast periods show a profitable return. A negative result may also be acceptable when, through a considered decision, you have spent in excess on an expense item to achieve an improved long- term result. Otherwise, a negative Profit result is unacceptable and must trigger immediate remedial action.

Positive 'actual' profit results, even for successive periods, will not necessarily mean that you have available cash. A payment of cash, thus reducing some long-term debt, may have been made. Remember, in the Financial Analysis, I have recorded Sales. Sales are Product sold and delivered and/or Services rendered. These are shown in the Profit and Loss Account as Sales for that period. However, you may not have been paid for those sales, in part or in whole. It may be that in your business, you have given clients credit and/ or are operating on extended terms such as thirty days from receipt of invoice, as an example. It is a common expression of confusion to identify a profit result only to have less cash available than the Profit indicates. But where is the money? I have heard many executives ask this in consternation. There are many reasons why the available cash does not equate to the calculated Profit results. However, both the available cash and the financial profit result may well be both absolutely correct. The disparity between the two aspects is caused mainly through situations such as the following:

- Product component and material supplies may have been purchased and paid ahead of requirement, thereby using cash for the acquisition of goods pertaining to future sales. This variation would be reflected in the Balance Sheet but not necessarily in the Profit and Loss Account. Excessive stocks of materials, products, or componentry are a common cause of cash unplanned usage and, therefore, cash shortage. Hence, it is never automatically wise to purchase large quantities of anything because of attractive prices. Always analyse the situation first, being aware of the cost of cash shortages. It is unwise to invest in long-term excess stocks saving, say 5% on the normal purchase price, only to incur a bank overdraft for that cash at, say, 10%, or to incur increased storage costs in excess of the saving or to risk old and redundant stock as a result of sales changes.
- Debtors extending over the close of any period under analysis will cause cash that should be in our possession for sales provided but has not yet been paid through extended credit, bad debts etc... This is not shown in the Profit and Loss

Account but is recorded as an overall debt in the Asset section of the Balance Sheet, to be explained in the following.

- Creditors to whom you may owe cash for product or services provided may not have been paid at the close of the period in question, thus inflating your cash reserves. Creditors are not shown in the Profit and Loss Account but are recorded as a Liability in the Balance Sheet, to be explained in the following.

- Long-term borrowings against which period (monthly) payments are made and which consist of principal and interest. Only the interest paid is shown in the Profit and Loss Account, whilst the paid principal shows in a reduction of the debt recorded in the Liability section of the Balance Sheet, explained in the following. Therefore, the cash paid against the principal of a loan will not be reflected in the Profit and Loss Account, resulting in negative a difference between the Profit and the Cash available.

- Capital expenditure: Equipment purchased for the business of an appreciable size will be recorded as an asset in the Balance Sheet and does not appear in the Profit and Loss Account. This expenditure remains as an item in the Balance Sheet and is subject to depreciation, thus reducing the asset from time to time. The Balance Sheet Asset entry is increased as equipment or other large acquisition occurs. As the depreciation is determined, it is recorded as an expense in the Profit and Loss Account and a commensurate decrease in the Assets factor of Equipment in the Balance Sheet. The function of applying depreciation is usually within the realm of the accountant and is not a subject for inclusion in this guide. However, sufficient to say, and as explained, the cash used for the purchase of the Capital Expenditure is not shown in the Profit and Loss Account.

- Extraneous loans to and from the business: From time to time, you may decide, through circumstances real or imagined, to obtain additional cash from the business for private use. Or it may be necessary to inject cash from a private source, such as you, into the business. These cash transactions are recorded in the Balance Sheet as Loans to a Director as an asset or Loans from a Director as a liability. Neither is recorded into the Profit and Loss Account and, therefore, will adversely or otherwise affect the available cash.

- Theft: There are many causes of cash variation between the actual cash available and the profit shown in the Profit and Loss Account. However, as these causes are eliminated without resolution for the difference, it may become a suspicion that theft and pilferage has occurred. Always be aware of the temptation that is open to staff and indeed yourself. It is so easy to use business cash in the belief that after all, it is your money and you work hard, so why can't you have it. Unless every movement of cash is recorded, and for whatever reason, you will waste much time in needless investigation. Pilferage is perhaps the major reason for shortages and for which staff may be responsible. And of course your own forays into the till.

13.6 Profit and Loss Review and Correction

A formal review of the Profit and Loss Account should be applied regularly and often. Be aware that this takes time and can be done too frequently. I suggest a monthly review is ideal, although a quarterly review once the business seems to be operating satisfactorily may be acceptable. Anything less frequent is fraught with danger, whilst anything more frequent may be bureaucratic, time consuming and meaningless.

A review will mean an examination of the 'actual' results of each and every entry in the Profit and Loss statement over the most recent operative period. Both positive and negative results should be examined and resolved.

CHAPTER 14

CAPITAL EXPENDITURE BUDGET

You are now ready to plan for any equipment, machinery, and business aid you will need and when. Depending on the product or service you have planned to involve with your business, you will need an analysis to identify the items required in order to provide the products and services you plan to market, with due regard to a realistic time frame. As with the expansion and development you have planned, additional equipment will be required, and this provision and timing will need to be established. All this Capital Expenditure budgeting will need to be included in your Cash Flow budgeting, to be discussed later.

As an example, the following table indicates a typical Capital Expenditure budget. I would only plan, in this instance, for twelve months ahead. If, during the twelve months, large items of capital are envisaged, planning can be done at that stage. This is a safer strategy because at that stage, you will have an idea how the entire business planning is tracking with your initial plans.

CAPITAL EXPENDITURE BUDGET: 1ST YEAR

		Pre Start	1st quarter	2nd Quarter	3rd Quarter	4th Quarter	Annual Total
			AUD $	AUD $	AUD $	AUD $	AUD $
Office							
	Chairs 3	400	0	0	0	0	400
	Desks 2	800	0	0	0	0	800
	Storage 1	200	200	0	0	0	400
	Filing Cabinet 2	170	0	0	0	0	170
	Computers 3	2500	1500	0	0	0	4000
	Software	800	600	0	0	0	1400
	Telephone	800	0	0	0	0	800
	Other	1500	0	0	0	0	1500
Transport							
	Car	30000	0	0	0	0	30000
	Truck	20000	0	0	0	0	20000
Factory							
	Hand tools	150	100	0	0	0	250
	Lathe	500	0	0	0	0	500
	Assembly benches	1500	1000	0	0	0	2500
	Assembly fixtures	3500	1500	0	0	0	5000
Total		62500	4900	0	0	0	67500

CHAPTER 15

BALANCE SHEET

The Balance Sheet completes the simple financial control documentation with which you will initially be involved. The Profit and Loss Account details the activity situation of the business over a set period of time. The Cash Flow details the actual cash available or expected to be available at any point in time. However, this will be discussed at a later time in this guide.

The Balance Sheet shows the total financial situation of the business at a selected point in time. I will discuss a simple Balance Sheet as shown in the following. It is not necessarily important that you create a Balance Sheet on a regular basis as it is usually the domain of your accountant. However, it will indicate the worth of the business at a certain date, although should you need to close the business for any reason, the Balance Sheet does not show the accurate value of the business. Stock and equipment would need to be sold off usually at a much reduced price, thus affecting the overall business value. Other Financial Formulae are determinable, adjusting the Balance Sheet to more practical and timely dimensions, for this eventuality. For the purpose of this exercise, the following example is sufficient to demonstrate the function and determination of the Balance Sheet.

		Balance Sheet after First 12 Months' Operation		
Assets				
	Cash	59,983		
	Debtors	66,027	Refer P&L Forecast	
	Equipment	67,500	Refer Capital Expense Budget	
	Subtotal	**193,510**		
Liability				
	Creditors	0		
	Loan Short-Term	0		
	Loan Long-Term	150,000	**Bank Loan**	
	Subtotal	**150,000**		
Net Assets/Liabilities		**43,510**		
Owner's Investment		150,000		
Retained Earnings		43,510		
		193,510		

CHAPTER 16

CASH FLOW

Knowing the situation of your cash balance at any given time is an essential element of business control. You may well have experienced good trading results providing positive net profits, but this should not be interpreted as available cash. There are many reasons for this, all of which you should maintain awareness.

Your net trading profit might show a positive result, but this can be rapidly consumed through outstanding debtors. Outstanding debtors are sales for which you have not received payment. Outstanding debtors are not revealed on the Profit and Loss Statement. So let us assume that you have achieved record sales, resulting in your analysis showing a profit of, say, $50,000, but these sales have not yet been paid, and thus, your outstanding debtors are totalling, say, $75,000, then your available cash is less than your expectations by $25,000. This could cause extreme embarrassment and even foreclosure.

In a similar yet opposite example, you might not have paid for your product purchases, other operating commitments, or outstanding expenses. Product purchases usually can demand thirty- day trading terms, and this will result in a belief that there is more cash available than a reconciled position will reveal.

All these types of examples, and more, too numerous to mention here, will cause you to have more or less cash in hand than there rightly should be, creating an incorrect premise that may result in incorrect and irresponsible spending decisions.

Therefore, a current cash-flow analysis is essential for effective and safe business control. Computer programs will make this analysis readily simple. Again, it may be wise to wait until you are capable with manual application before embarking on a computerised program. A monthly analysis spreadsheet should be created, showing all 'cash out', 'cash in', and cash available or 'balance' expectations. This will reveal cash available and the amount of cash required now and into the future. This analysis is a 'must' for bank financial assistance. Whilst I have encouraged an accurate and possibly mildly optimistic forecasting effort throughout this text, cash flow analyses should reflect a practical yet minimal pessimistic view. It should be done on a monthly basis, and while I have shown a cash flow in quarterly segments, this is only for demonstration purposes.

In the simple Cash Flow example following, the various segments are explained, and this format can be readily applied, both manually or through one of the many computer programs available. Whilst I have shown, therefore, in the example quarterly segments, in practice, it is preferable to use monthly segments.

An 'actual' column should be created alongside each quarter or segment, thus enabling the actual situation to be recorded and, therefore, reviewed at the close of each period.

Opening Balance

The initial entry should show the amount of cash in hand, or cash available to the business in the bank, at the commencement of the first period. Subsequent 'Opening Balances' will reflect the calculated final estimated balance from the previous period.

Income. This should show all expected income, under separate subheadings such as creditor payments, loan repayments, interest received into the business etc…

Creditor payments represent cash received for sales. This may be cash received immediately for a sale, cash received as a result of thirty-day trading, and this is usually received in the month following the sale, and overdue cash received for past sales. Using a conservative approach, it is usual to assume that all sales will be paid in the following month, although you may consider it worthy to delay some percentage of these payments into the following month. This is particularly so, where you may have approved extended credit. In the following example, where quarterly segments have been applied, I have assumed all sales will be paid in the quarter following the sale. This estimate, naturally, is very conservative, as some will be paid in the same period when the sales occurred. However, you must be aware also that some payments will be late and may occur in the second, and possibly third, period following the sales. Therefore, use your best forecast and enter payment for sales in the quarter in which you expect to receive the payment.

I have estimated that 2/3rd of the first quarter sales will be paid during the first quarter. That is during the second and third months of the first quarter. Payment for the remaining one month of the first quarter sales will be received together with the payment for two months of the second quarter sales, during the second quarter. A similar formula has been applied for the third quarter and fourth quarters. This leaves one month of the fourth quarter sales unpaid at the end of the twelve-month period.

Should there be any further income from other sources such as interest from business investments, which is realised in cash, this should also be shown in the Income column when the payments are expected.

Subtotal. This will show the subtotal of all cash income for each period.

Payments. This should record all cash outgoings for the purchase of capital equipment, stock, services, componentry, and materials which are used or intended for use in producing a final product or service for sale and any other cash that may be spent for the purposes of investment, loans etc.

Again, in this category, not all purchases will be paid in the period in which the goods are acquired. You may use approved extended credit, in which case, the outgoing cash should only be recorded in the period in which it is actually paid. Similarly, cash may be paid, in some circumstances, before the product or equipment is received, such as for international orders. Thus, in the following example, product has been purchased before the period in which it is required, and I have applied extended credit of thirty-day terms for that product purchased. Therefore, the cash outlay for purchased product is shown in the period in which it is used even though it was acquired in the previous period. Conversely, I have allowed for immediate payment for the capital equipment purchased, as it is doubtful whether credit would be available for the acquisition of equipment at this early stage.

Direct labour wages must be paid in the period in which they are used, and therefore, I have shown the cash payment of Direct Labour for manufacturing and service in the same section as shown in the Profit and Loss Account, Cost of Sales section, and indeed in the same period in which they are paid.

Subtotal. A subtotal of the purchases and payments will show those cash outgoings paid for, all costs involved with the Cost of Sales during the period in which they are, or are planned to be, paid.

Expenses. The individual allocations of cash outgoings in this section should accommodate all other expenditure and should correspond with those shown in the Profit and Loss Account. However, while the Profit and Loss account will show entries for expense committed in a certain period, the Cash Flow entry should only reflect that cash that is estimated to be actually paid in each period. Whilst the total twelve month figure for any allocation may or may not equal the Profit and Loss Account total for that classification, the individual period entries will most probably differ, depending when you estimate the payment will be made.

Total expense. A total of the expense allocations will show the estimated total expenses for each period.

Total payments. The Payments subtotal added to the Expense total will show the Total Payments estimated to be made for each period.

Cash balance. The Total Payments subtracted from the Total Income for each segment will show the estimated Cash Balance for each period. This cash balance should be transferred to the next period as the Opening Balance for that next period.

This Cash Flow will show the cash situation at the close of each period or at any intermediate time of your choosing. It will indicate how much cash is required to create and establish your business and prove a necessity when negotiating financial assistance from banks or other providers. It will indicate when the expected business profits will be recognised as available cash and when the business can afford to acquire equipment, additional labour, or expenditure of any kind. It will clarify the difference between profit and available cash. However, forecasting cash flow is only as accurate as your operational budgeted forecasts. Therefore, if sales are less than expected or if expenditure is higher than forecast or if the purchases of materials and product and the basic costs of these purchases are higher than planned and if debtors are higher or slower in paying than planned, then the available cash will be less than forecast. Conversely, if you are operating better than forecast in some or all these areas, not only the profits as shown in the Profit and Loss account but also the available cash will be better than forecast.

The Cash Flow forecast is an invaluable tool for forecasting your viability and control, and without such an analysis, one would be heading for financial disaster.

Cash Flow Forecast

		Note that Cash Flow should be calculated by month.					
		To do this, monthly budgets and expenditure are required.					
	Comments	Pre Start	1st Quarter	2nd Quarter	3rd Quarter	4th Quarter	
Opening Balance		150,000	87,400	51,555	37,240	35,005	59,983
Income	Assume 30 Day Payment		16,560	42,200	73,320	121,773	
Subtotal		150,000	103,960	93,755	110,560	156,778	
Payments							

Capital Invest	Refer Capital Expenditure Budget	62,600	4,900	0	0	0	
Purchases	Assume each Quarter Requirements Acquired Pre-Quarter and Paid. 30 Day. Refer Product Requirement Summary		4,625	9,750	16,000	21,250	
Direct Labour			5,725	11,450	24,400	39,250	
Subtotal		62,600	15,250	21,200	40,400	60,500	
Expenses							

	Accountant			300		600	
	Advertising		90	0	50	60	
	Bank or Financier Charges		50	50	50	50	
	Car Expenses						
	Fuel		60	50	50	40	
	Insurance		700	0	0	0	
	Licence		150	0	0	0	
	Registration		600	0	0	0	
	Repairs			60	120	420	
	Service			150	150	200	
	Computers		100		250	150	
	Govt. Charges			120		180	
	Innovation			100		100	
	Insurance		800				
	Mail		120	60	60	60	
	Power		200	180	180	140	
	Rental		1,375	1,375	1,375	1,375	

	Security		110	110	110	110	
	Stationary		100	60	60	60	
	Telephone		100	100	100	150	
	Wages						
	Self		17,600	17,600	17,600	17,600	
	Staff		15,000	15,000	15,000	15,000	
Total Expense			37,155	35,315	35,155	36,295	
Total Payments		62,600	52,405	56,515	75,555	96,795	
Cash Balance		87,400	51,555	37,240	35,005	59,983	
Notes	For this business, one would require access from oneself, or either bank or financier, of $150,000.						
	Recoupment of the original capital begins in 4th quarter, finishing 1st year of operation with $59,983 ($60,000) of the original $150,000 outlay.						

An analysis of this cash flow will show that although it would seem that after the first year of operation there is only $60,000 of the original $150,000 left, there are $66,000 of outstanding debtors. Therefore, the first year of establishment and operation is forecast to have cost, in real terms, $24,000, and this includes the capital investment of $67,500 on equipment.

16.1 Bank Assistance

Equipped with the Profit and Loss Account Forecast, the Cash Flow Forecast, and the documentation making up the Strategic Plan, all of which you have developed whilst working through this guide, you are now in a position of relative strength to approach the bank or a financier. You are now confidently aware of the amount of finance you need, when you need, and for how long. Unless you personally own the necessary finance, you will need to acquire funding. There is no option. Providing you have done the planning work correctly and in detail, finance should be readily available.

Review and identify a number of opportunities where a contact for funding may be made. Don't limit yourself to just one provider. You will need to compare costs, interest rates, and conditions of finance. Once you have approval, there is nothing that can stop you from embarking on the path of development with your business.

You may identify a potential partner who, for some recognition such as a percentage of the business, will offer finance. This can often be attractive, but a word of warning to encourage you to exercise caution: at this early stage, it may be unwise to share your business with persons or organisations whose only interest will be to share your profits.

16.2 Bank Overdraft Facilities

During the course of your business, the cash flow will fluctuate in relation to the state of the various and numerous business disciplines. Therefore, at times you will, in all probability, require a short-term injection of funds. It is difficult and time-consuming to approach the bank or a financier each time this occurs. It may be opportune to approach the bank or a financier for an overdraft facility of, say, $30,000, depending entirely upon your previous assumptions and planning calculations. If approved, this will attract a small interest or facility charge. In the event that you need to use some of the overdraft facility, there will be no need for additional or timely applications and approvals. It is satisfactory to merely draw on the overdraft facility, at which time you will be charged interest for the amount you have drawn. Early repayment will negate the need for continuing interest charges.

CHAPTER 17

CHEQUE AND CASH CONTROL

It is common practice to utilise several means of receiving and storing cash and paying cash for product or services provided to the business.

Cash or any other means of income, which may be received from debtors, should be banked, thus establishing a strong record of all income. Cash, cheques, bank transfers, and electronic transfers are all popular methods of receiving payment.

This receipt of cash should be immediately recorded, receipt issued, and the payment documented against the debtors details. Thus, at any time, one can identify the state of debtors and the elapsed time of the debt.

Cash is usually held for minor operative purchases as 'Petty Cash'. The Petty Cash is funded periodically, as required, from the main area of cash funding. Records of petty cash spending should be maintained, reviewed, and approved on a regular basis. Petty Cash drawings should be recorded as expense outgoings in the Profit and Loss Account. Therefore, at any time, a review can identify the petty cash spending in general from the Profit and Loss Account and the petty cash detailed spending from the recorded regular review.

Creditor payments can be made by cash, cheque, bank, or electronic transfer. It is wise to limit cash payments, as unless accurate records are maintained, it is difficult to track a past payment.

Cheques issued for creditor payments must be recorded and the cheque situation regularly reconciled.

Note that all payments received—whether in cash, cheque, or bank transfer—must be recorded against the creditor file, therefore establishing a record in the Profit and Loss Account.

CHAPTER 18

CREDIT CONTROL

At all times, you must be aware of the client's business stability and credit rating, either formally or by reputation, before you extend credit terms. Although, if the reputation of the client is only through hearsay, extreme care should be applied. The attraction of orders, at times large orders, will encourage you to take the risk of providing credit. Never succumb to temptation. A lost sale is better than lost cash through non-payment for goods and services. Depending on the type of business and size of the operation, you may demand credit terms, but always establish a credit rating before this is granted. Alternatively, an appreciable deposit can, to some extent, allay your fears.

18.1 Creditor Control

This is often a neglected aspect of business control. Either through cash shortage or consideration that a late payment will be permitted by the supplier, many consider that suppliers can wait for payment for their goods or services. This is absolutely incorrect. Whilst a creditor remains unpaid for goods and services you have legitimately received and, worse still, unrecorded, you will not have accurate reports regarding your business activity. More particularly, invoices *must* be recorded immediately when they are received and matched up with previously recorded order commitments, irrespective of whether or when those accounts have been, or are intended to be, paid. Only in this manner will you recognise your current business position. Similarly, as soon as the invoices are paid, the payment must be recorded. Whether this is done manually in the documentation you have set up or in a computer program specifically acquired for the business records, only with conscious timely recording of all transactions will the business records accurately reflect the business position.

Regular payment of suppliers' invoices on time will create a reputation for timely payments. Should you, at any future time, need some extension of credit, the suppliers may be inclined to provide leniency as a result of your past performances.

18.2 Supplier's Invoices/Statements

On several occasions, I have found current unpaid and unrecorded invoices and statements held in obscure files, even sometimes stuffed into overflowing desk drawers and only removed after a shuffling process to decide which invoice to pay. This shuffling decision was often influenced by the more aggressive creditor at the time these late-payment records were documented. However, this was too late to reflect business, cash, and creditor liabilities, and the risk of supply stoppages and possible foreclosure was always imminent.

Invoices received should be immediately recorded in order to ensure that your business records are current and do not reflect an incorrect position. More importantly, you should not forget, or otherwise ignore, a supplier's invoice for payment.

Always endeavour to pay creditors within the arranged and established credit terms. This is usually 30-day terms in the business arena, although longer terms can always be negotiated once you have earned business credibility. If, through cash shortage, it is difficult to meet payment commitments, always discuss the situation with the supplier, endeavouring to obtain an easing of payment conditions.

Maintain an open dialogue with your creditors. This policy establishes excellent credit relationships and opens the door to future leniency.

18.30 Debtor Control

It is imperative to initiate and control your debtors. Establish at the beginning what payment terms you require. Of course, the ideal would be immediate cash payment for all your sales, whether they are product or services. However, it may be an accepted practice, and usually is, to provide 30-day terms of payment. This means that any sales you make within a calendar month will be invoiced, either immediately after the sale is made or at the end of the month. Payment is usually expected by the end of the ensuing month. So if your invoice is one day late and reaches your client in the following month, it may not be paid until the end of the second month. This could be up to almost three months after the sale. Your business cash flow could not support this type of credit terms, particularly during the initial periods of business creation.

Always create and present your invoice to the client, either at the time of sale or at some period well before the close of the month in which the sale is made. This should provide the payment for that sale in the month following the sale. However, depending on your style of business, and on the credibility of the client, you may adopt a cash-sale policy, thereby establishing a cash business. In any event, ensure that your invoice design includes your payment policy and any penalty that may be applied, should payment be late. Your legal adviser or accountant could advise on this. Care in this aspect must be applied as unnecessary restrictive conditions and blunt demands can cause loss of sales.

Always review your debtor list at the close of each month, creating a list detailing the status whether it is current, 30-day, 60-day, or 90-day and greater. This is of utmost importance and should not be delayed or overlooked.

The collection of overdue accounts is a function that is not enjoyed by business owners, especially in the early periods of the business development, although there are not many proprietors who ever feel really comfortable with collection of overdue accounts. However, it must be done, and there is no easy way. Ask for your money outright, leaving no opportunity for misunderstanding. The client is the one who should be embarrassed and under an obligation. Be prepared to offer terms but only if absolutely necessary. The collection of overdue accounts can often be an opportunity for additional sales or, at least, for firming a relationship with your client. It may be that after some period of accumulating bad and poor debts, you consider the employ of a debt-collecting agency. For a percentage fee, this type of collection usually returns some recompense, although the employment of a debt collector will almost certainly lose the client.

CHAPTER 19

FINANCIAL FORMULAE

At times, in the life of a business, it is desirable to measure the financial stability and operational effectiveness of a business. For these purposes, there have been established several Financial Ratios. These are usually left to the domain of an accountant and are not regularly required for the daily operation and control of a small business. Of the many Financial Ratios, some are more applicable to the small business proprietor than others. They are useful indicators of a business performance and financial situation. Most Financial Ratios can be calculated from the business financial reports that have been previously discussed in this guide. They can be used to analyse business trends and to compare the business progress against those of the competitors and industry benchmarks. A few of the more popular Financial Ratios are described in the following, but this is only for information and comprehension of that which is available, rather than as a guide to a detailed knowledge for your regular implementation.

Cost of Sales to Sales. This ratio measures the actual cost of the products, services, and direct labour used for the sales achieved in a given period. It includes all the costs directly involved in the purchase and/or production of a product. Or in the situation of a Service, it includes all direct costs involved with that service. Therefore, this Direct Labour factor can be a comparison that can involve the measure for an audit and ongoing control of the supplier's pricing on the internal efficiency of manufacturing and servicing. Should a supplier's prices increase, this ratio will increase, and the Gross Profit (following) will decrease. Similarly, should your manufacturing efficiency decrease, this ratio will increase, and the Gross Profit (following) will decrease. Thus, should this ratio increase, your first areas of investigation should be your supplier's prices and your manufacturing efficiency. Steps should, therefore, be taken without delay to correct the situation by negotiating better pricing of goods and attention given to a return to your expected and pre-determined manufacturing efficiency.

Gross Profit Margin

This is a measure of the gross profit earned on sales. It considers the cost of goods or services that have been sold only and does not consider other costs identified as expenses or overheads. Therefore, it is only a measure of the profitability of each product. It doesn't tell you whether your business is making a profit overall. For that measurement, you need the Net Profit Ratio. However, in conjunction with the Cost of Sales Ratio, it is an important surveillance to control the profitability at this point of your analysis.

Gross Profit = Sales—Cost of Sales Gross Profit Margin = Gross Profit / Sales

Depending on the industry in which your business is involved, the Gross Profit margin will vary, but your resultant margin should approximate that recognised as the normal percentage return by similar businesses in your industry. It can, therefore, become a valuable tool for comparison when measuring the effectiveness of your business. However, as mentioned previously, you must include the state of your expenses or overheads in order to accurately compare your business profitability.

Expenses (overhead) to Sales

This ratio is a measurement of all overhead expenses, meaning all expenses other than those included in the Cost of Sales, compared with the actual sales for a given period of time. It is a continuing challenge for you, as the Proprietor, to continually find ways in which to achieve reductions in this area of expense. A reduction in Expenses will directly increase your Net Profitability. An intense regular examination of each and every allocation of expense to identify reduction opportunities will produce increased profits, or a return to profitability. Therefore, a less-than-acceptable profit result should cause an immediate examination of the expense allocations. Reasons for overspending will sometimes satisfy your analysis, but a correction should be your aim. It is relatively easy to have excuses for excessive spending on Expenses. However, one must take a blind attitude towards overspending and endeavour, through responsible analysis, to sensibly reduce any overspending and return to, or even reduce further, from the budgeted amount.

Net Profit Margin

This ratio is the difference between the Gross Profit (calculated) and the Expenses (calculated) compared with the Sales for any given period, reduced to a percentage figure. This is a quick manner of reference to determine the profitability of your business. It will provide a satisfactory comparable measurement between periods, thus enabling you to determine the trend of your business.

Net Profit Margin = Gross Profit – Expenses / Sales x 100

Note that the foregoing Ratios relate to a specific length of time of business trading and reflect how your business has operated over a given period.

The following Ratios relate to the Balance Sheet and reflect the state of your business at any predetermined point in time.

Current Ratio

You may be making profits but are not realising sufficient profit to meet your liabilities. The Current Ratio assists you to measure the solvency of your business by comparing your Current Assets (unpaid sales invoices) to your Current Liabilities (unpaid accounts and the like). The Current Ratio is the ratio between Current Assets and Current Liabilities. This ratio is of particular interest to a financier who may be considering a short-term credit for the business. A high-current ratio reflects a business's capability to meet its short-term financial obligations. However, a low-Current Ratio may indicate to the proprietor and shareholders that the business assets are being used to grow the business. The Current Ratio indicates the ability of the business to remain liquid after paying all of its debts. However, this includes all items such as long-term loans, and debts as liabilities, and inventory which may be difficult to sell off quickly. It would also include items such as equipment and other similar capital investment items which would not necessarily return the depreciated Balance Sheet value.

Quick Ratio

This is also referred to as the Liquid Ratio or Acid Test. It measures the ability of a business to utilise its immediate or ready cash or assets that can be turned to cash quickly, close to their book value, in order to meet all its Current Liabilities immediately. Therefore, it necessarily follows that a business that has a Quick Ratio of less than one cannot pay back its Current Liabilities without delay.

The common formula for determining the Quick Ratio is as follows:

Quick Action Ratio = Current Assets $—Inventories $/Current Liabilities $

Inventory or stock is omitted from the financial sum of the assets. It is considered less than probable that the business could convert the stock value to cash quickly.

The quick ratio is more conservative than the current ratio but is considered a more well-known liquidity measure because it excludes inventory from current assets. Inventory is excluded because some companies have difficulty turning their inventory into cash. In the event that short- term obligations need to be paid off immediately, there are situations in which the Current Ratio would overestimate a company's short-term financial strength.

Inventory Turnover

This measurement will only affect your business operational audit if you need to carry trading stock or inventory to satisfy the demands of your clientele. It shows how many times your finished stock business inventory is sold and replaced over a given period. The ratio compares the value of the cost of goods sold over a given period with the value at cost of the stock in hand at the close of that period. So if you have sold at cost $100,000 worth of goods over the preceding month, and you currently have $200,000 worth of goods at cost in stock, then the Inventory Turnover is 0.5 per month.

The higher this figure, the more efficient is the use of your cash, and it necessarily follows that the lower the figure, the more cash you have tied up in stock. For example, in the example, where the resultant figure compute to 1, then it would mean that you had $100,000 of goods in stock to satisfy a month's sales of $100,000, thereby releasing $100,000 cash.

Inventory Turnover can be calculated as—
Sales at cost $ / Inventory at cost $

It can also be calculated as—
Cost of Goods Sold $ / Average Inventory at cost $

The days in the period can then be divided by the inventory turnover formula to calculate the days it takes to sell the inventory on hand or 'Inventory Turnover Days'.

Return on Owner's Equity

Return on Owner's Equity compares your net business income to the equity you have invested in the business. It reveals how much you are making from your investment.

If you have invested $200,000 in the business, and your net profit is $50,000, then the return on your equity in the business is 25%.

Return on Owner's Equity = Net Income / Owner's equity

CHAPTER 20

CORRECTIVE ACTION

Once your business is under way and operating, bring this discipline into play. It is the most important function of your ongoing business, and it will provide a direct road to quality and excellence in performance.

Quality of product or service is not the best you can offer nor is it the best possible outcome. It may be, but it is not necessarily so. Quality of product and service is the absolute conformance with documented specifications and written expectations. So to improve a product or service, we must first determine how they are to be improved and document that improvement. In this manner, staff may be encouraged and trained to ensure that every product and service produced for the client is absolutely in conformance with the documented specification. The best way this can be achieved is through this procedure of Corrective Action.

Every problem encountered in business, whether externally or internally generated, that is recognised as a problem, is an opportunity for long-term correction. This applies to product, service, internal activities, staff misadventures, or indeed anything that may happen to go wrong during the activities of the business. Each correction of a problem which should include a procedural change or amendment is a positive improvement in the quality of your business operation. Complete excellence of quality of service and product and operation can never be achieved. It is a continuous improvement programme towards quality that will place your business at the forefront of your industry, profession, or business affairs. Never ignore Customer Complaints. Whether internal or external, they are the prime means of improvement. Give a little thought as to who is the customer. A customer is both internal and external, indeed anyone who is connected with the daily operation of the business. Externally are those persons such as customers, advisers, government and industry officials, and anyone else who may not be employed by the business but is involved in some way with the general operation. Internally are those employees at any level who may make mistakes, may have ideas for improved operation, or who may have been inadvertently involved in misdemeanours of product, service, or general actions. Conducted correctly, there are numerous examples of this correction factor applying to all these areas.

20.1 Problem Reporting and Review

Unless you identify and recognise problems, when and where they occur, and prevent them from happening again, your business will stagnate and suffer from repeated mistakes and client problems. Many business owners have encouraged me to believe that their business does not have problems, and any that may arise from time to time are corrected by them personally and do not reoccur. This type of belief is a fallacy and leads to failure and poor quality.

All problems, whether internal staff problems, business procedural problems, client-related problems, or product/service problems, must be identified without favour, guilt, defensiveness, or blame. It is only at this stage that correction can be applied with the resultant continual quality improvement.

20.2 Procedural Correction

Problems, which must include suggestions for improvements, can be identified in many ways. They may arise from staff complaints about any number and manner of subjects. They may arise from either operational errors and product—or service-related difficulties, or client complaints and suggestions.

Whatever they may be, they must be recorded. Such recording medium must be available to all concerned persons. It is common to establish a centrally or conveniently located document, either a book or a suitably identified sheet. This should be available to all staff and clientele and will show date, problem, and an area for the entry of a reviewed reply. It need not show the identification of the person entering the problem, although most times, this is included.

This record of problems must be regularly reviewed by you or your responsible representative. The review may result in a decision not to react to the recorded problem. This must be your decision, and such decision may be made because you consider the problem too trivial or that it may not repeat through circumstances of which you are aware. However, you must not disregard the problem flippantly as many are encouraged to do. In most instances, you will recognise a real problem and determine, either individually or through a group, a correction that will ensure that the problem will never reoccur. Thus, you will have established a continuous improvement factor. This should be recorded into the initial documentation. Having determined a correction, a Procedure should be created and included in the formal documented procedures for the business. The relevant staff should be trained in the application of the new procedure. The Complaint Register must be ruled off, indicating that a review of the entries has been made and a short response documented to each entry. This will show all who read the register that a complaint has been reviewed and a correction has or has not been initiated.

External entries must be considered as explained, and the person who recorded the incident or complaint must be notified of the result. This action must be recorded into the Complaints Register for all to see.

Such is the practice of recognising complaints from all sources, reviewing each case with a positive mind, implementing a correction being mindful of the cost and applicability, and recording the outcome for all to see. This is the prime mover of quality and continuous improvement, and all actions will be converted to a positive result on the bottom line.

CHAPTER 21

BUSINESS DISCIPLINES

In recent decades, businesses have been required in certain circumstances to formalise their business procedures in accordance with approved national and international Standards. In many instances, this formalisation was a requirement in order to be considered for large contracts, either governmental or of private selection. It was, therefore, considered, in many instances, a bureaucratic overkill and very paper-intense and expensive. Many businesses were innocently involved with drastic and costly effects. Subsequently, rationality prevailed, and the Standards being demanded merely outlined basic business common sense, which, when interpreted correctly, empowered those businesses involved, in continuous improvement and a common- sense search for excellence, coupled at all times with documented uniform and standard operations. Many businesses have advantaged themselves of this interpretation, resulting in improved and economical operations, competitive strength, and bottom line profits. Those generally internationally accepted and, therefore, popularly recognised standards are Quality, ISO 9001; Environment, ISO 14001; and Occupational Health, Welfare, and Safety. There are many more that can be implemented, depending upon the business direction.

Sufficient at this stage is to comment, as I have done, and to recommend that at a future stage, your business should address one or more of these disciplines. In that regard, it would be simpler and less expensive to become involved early in the development of your business, rather than later.

Implementation of the Standards should be simple, basic, and in accordance with your own business practices. Carried out in this manner will ensure that the implementation of the Standards will not interfere or disrupt the normal effective and efficient operation of your business. Indeed, if implemented correctly, simply, and in accordance with your business disciplines, you may find that the Standards will assist your general operation and inclusion of business principles.

CHAPTER 22

DOCUMENTATION

Through all the facets of business creation that this guide has thus far led you, there has been a continual reference to the necessary documentation of all your deliberations. This documentation is absolutely necessary, and you should have, by now, a dossier of planning and information documents, which, together, represent your Business Plan. This Business Plan will guide you as you develop your business. It will provide a professional and formal document for the relative financiers, such as banks, to judge your worth for financial assistance. It will provide a basis for regular revisiting and comparison with your actual results, thus encouraging attention to some lagging aspects, to amendment of the Plan where necessary and to update certain variances that may occur. It will facilitate an Action Plan in line with the documented requirements of the Plan for certain individuals, staff, and yourself to abide.

The Business Plan should be confidential and restricted to yourself, trusted staff of your selection, and any external involvements. The financial sections of the Plan should be further restricted to yourself and any financiers who may be required to review your situation.

By now your documentation is becoming quite extensive, although completely relevant. File it logically and safely in order that it may be recovered quickly and simply.

Allow me to put one scenario regarding documentation to you; this will entirely depend upon your business.

I consulted to a small business wherein there were several persons, all involved in receiving client's request and developing quotations for impending work. Over a relatively short period of time, the proprietor developed a standard series of letters and documents relating to the business activities. Whenever an employee was asked by a client for a certain offer or reassurance in writing, that letter created by the employee, would be reviewed by the proprietor and, if necessary, amended, and placed on file for future usage. Activities gradually developed to the stage that all letters directed to an external person, such as a client, had to be first reviewed by the proprietor. If satisfactory, the letter was placed on file for future usage. The business activities developed to the stage that no letter was compiled by staff. All correspondence was found through the pre-prepared files. Thus, when correspondence was required to be created for a client, such was located on file and printed out for posting. This has reduced the administrative staff extensively, whilst improving the quality of documentation and accuracy of quotations to a point of excellence. Subsequently, the profitability of the business increased to levels not previously recognised.

Perhaps worth considering as your business develops.

CHAPTER 23

OPERATIONS, BUDGETS, FINANCE, REVIEW, AND AMENDMENT

The financial budget you have created will define and guide most of your decision-making and will provide the confidence for you to continue with the development of the business. This will open the avenue for regular audit of your systems and the progress your business is making against the predetermined forecast. It will provide you with the tools to review, analyse, and determine continuing strategies for success. It will provide proof of professional planning and give associates and interested partners confidence to support your business.

The real key to maintaining conformity with the budget is the achievement of the Sales Budget. Any deficiencies in this area must be addressed without delay. This does not mean drastic immediate action, rather a considered analysis of the situation and the identification and implementation of correction applications to bring the Sales back into budgeted parameters. Importantly, Expenses must be controlled and reduced to maintain the percentage goals for profitability. This is not always possible, but every endeavour must be made to, at least, curtail spending until a return to budget is achieved.

Sales in excess of budget can also create a difficult problem, or series of problems, and each must receive similar urgent analysis and correction. Problems such as cash shortage caused through increased and unforeseen material purchases to meet the additional sales, staff increases required to provide the additional capacity, and the payment of additional wages will all seem catastrophic at the time, but analysis and controlled correction will return a stable business with profitable returns. Remember also that incoming cash for additional sales will not be received for between thirty and sixty days. However, these are good problems and will provide additional profit to that budgeted.

The maintenance of 'Actual Performances', documented as discussed, will permit the realisation of increasing budget accuracy, with resultant smoother business operation.

Budget and Actual Performance regular review must never be stalled. It is most important that you remain acutely aware of the Sales versus Actual and the profitability of the business at all times. Include your staff in the reviews, thus gaining their confidence and support. Such may reduce the risk of non-conformances occurring.

CHAPTER 24

ACTION PLAN

An analysis of the entire Strategic Plan, and each ongoing review of that plan, will identify activities that need to be addressed and corrected to conform to the plan and the correction of all misadventures that may occur from time to time. These activities and the required correction must be listed and each item allocated to a person for action. Timing for the completion of each activity must be shown and all involved persons made aware of their individual requirements that are listed in the Action Plan. At regular intervals, the Action Plan should be reviewed to ensure that the desired activities have been completed as scheduled or are well on the way to completion.

Regular review of the Action Plan is essential thus ensuring that those functions allocated for correction to certain individuals have been corrected or are well on the way to so being. This will advantage the business in two distinct ways. First, it will ensure that errors and mishaps are corrected and, if applicable, new and revised procedures are issued and in place. These in themselves will provide a measure of continuous improvement. Secondly, the review function will cause the staff to be aware of the importance of the review and also of the need for definitive correction where advised.

CHAPTER 25

DISASTER PLAN

This is merely a precautionary function and one that I would hope is never required to be applied. It need not be considered immediately or before you commence your business. However, it is a subject that should be addressed in the early stages of your business development and consolidation. To be prepared often eases the stress and possible incorrect decision-making at a difficult time. At the time of business planning and creation, enthusiasm will usually reign supreme and overshadow most of your potentially negative thoughts. However, all too often, it seems the budgeted plans may not be achieved or shortages and malfunctions in operation may indicate that it will not be achieved. You must be prepared for this eventuality and have a plan formulated, detailing the action and result you would apply. Such a plan may address the following:

- Sales—How can more be obtained? How will you deal with a drop in sales to a poor level?
- Product or service—Will you need to amend or change the range offered to the market?
- Staff—Is the staff effective, and do you need to provide training or replacement?
- Location—Are you marketing to the correct geographical area and clientele?
- Supply—Are your suppliers reliable and competitive?

- Cash—Do you need cash, and is it available economically?
- Associates—Will you consider the viability of associates, either physically or financially?
- Last resort—At what stage will you cease trading and save whatever can be saved?

These are just a few suggestions that may be considered in a disaster plan, should it ever be necessary to take timely action to save, or cease, trading.

CHAPTER 26

INSURANCES

Professional Indemnity Insurance will be necessarily required as your business develops. Consider the risks while dealing with the public; mistakes, errors in interpretation, theft, and accidents may all require protection through formalised Insurance. Research of this aspect will best be served through investigations conducted with several insurance companies offering this cover.

As with all insurance, you may never use it, but it is a necessary factor. Refusal to gain cover could find you being sued for thousands of dollars for some minor variation in your business activities.

CHAPTER 27

SUMMARY

Having used the information in this guide to develop the various programmes, you should have, by now, accumulated a complete strategic plan. You are, therefore, ready to implement the creation and ongoing control of your business.

The financial planning that you have done will show whether finance is required, and this may mean an approach to the bank or other finance providers.

This planning is not set in concrete and should become the basis for continual review and comparison with actual performances, including revision, where necessary.

There are obviously many additional aspects of business development and control that you will experience as you progress. This will bring continual challenges, and it may be that you need to consider the employment of expert assistance either with permanent staff or through external contractual providers.

Through the many areas of development, you will probably consider the task of forecasting most impractical. This is perfectly understandable in the early stages of business involvement, but remember that any forecast is better than none. The correction factors built in to the review analysis that must become a continual process will correct inaccuracies, and you will be surprised how accurate your forecasts can become after a relative few periods of forecasting.

The main issues for your continual attention are Sales and Expense Control, and both in combination will dictate the financial success of your business. As sales vary from the forecast, and they will, so expenses must be controlled accordingly, particularly when a downwards trend is realised. Lesser sales must incur reduced expenses in order to recover, if not achieve, the forecast profit. Increased sales over budget will present another group of problems such as available cash, capacity viability, and supply delays. All these problems can be solved with judgement, planning, and viable decision-making.

Good luck with your venture.

John L Bates. BA, FAIM, FAICD, 1932—Present
A brief summary of my credentials is as follows:

- Marine Engineer 1st Class unrestricted (Deep Sea) retired. Board of Trade Marine Section, 1953 to 1956.
- Operations Manager, South Australia Caltex Oil, Australia, Pty Ltd., 1956 to 1964.
- Extensive experience in the management of national and international business. SABCO Pty Ltd., Australia and Scotland, UK. Manufacturing Manager, Australia, 1966 to 1981. Managing Director, Scotland, UK branch, 1981 to 1986. Works Director, Australia, 1986 to 1988.
- Founder, 1988, of two major South Australian Companies, each now among the national leaders in their own particular fields of operation. John L. Bates & Associates Pty Ltd (business consulting company, 1988 to 2005, retired) and Total Quality Certification Services International Pty Ltd (JASANZ accredited). Both companies are still operating; JLB is a national leader, whilst TQCSI is an international leader and active in many countries.
- Founder of the only privately operated microbiology laboratory in South Australia (at the time): Adelaide Microbiology Service Pty Ltd.
- Diploma in Company Directorship, 1994.
- Fellow Australian Institute of Company Directors.
- Fellow Australian Institute of Management.
- Past Certified Management Consultant.
- Chairman of Directors of prominent South Australian manufacturing group of companies. Century Group of Companies, 1990-2010. Retired August 2010.
- Chairman of Directors John L. Bates & Associates Pty Ltd., 1988-2011, retired.
- Director, Total Quality Certification Services, 1995 to 2011, retired.

- Director, Cruising Yacht Club of South Australia, 2002-2007, retired.
- Official inspector, Marinas Association of Australia, Golden Anchor Awards, retired.
- Author autobiography published.
- Landscapes in Oil artist—40 years.
- Mozambique business consultancy. Preparing business for successful certification to international quality standards.
- USA Taft prison, California. Prepared for accreditation to ISO 9001-2000. Audited for successful attainment.
- Mozambique business training. Presented two-week course in Finance for Non-financial Executives—a course designed by me to familiarise participants with financial control of business and cost control philosophies.
- USA. Preparing incarceration facilities for international quality certification to international standards.
- New Zealand. Preparing companies for Certification to ISO 9001.
- Graduated in 2009 at UNISA for BA Aboriginal Studies with a second major in Australian Studies.
- Appointed Justice of the Peace, April 2010.

1. Consulting experience involved Board and management training/mentoring, business plans, operational system development such as quality, environmental and OH&S systems for certification to international standards, production planning, system auditing, and training courses in all the above. I pioneered the Quality Certification Programme for business in South Australia, quickly expanding nationally. I developed and presented many training courses in business excellence, including quality, financial control, cost control, and business planning. I have audited many businesses for operational disciplines, such as quality, environmental, OH&S, and general operating excellence. The number of

companies to whom I have consulted would number many scores—local, national, and international.

2. I continue to mentor new business and existing small business as required.

John L. Bates
July 2014

Reward is not a right,
But the result of dedication and effort.